10.95

RECIPE FOR
Reading

SECOND EDITION
Revised and Expanded

NINA TRAUB

SCHOOL PSYCHOLOGIST FOR THE OSSINING PUBLIC SCHOOLS
OSSINING, NEW YORK

with

FRANCES BLOOM

WALKER AND COMPANY ● **New York**

DEDICATION

This book is dedicated to Dr. John B. Murray C.N., Professor and Chairman of the Psychology Department of St. John's University in New York.

Dr. Murray is the author of seven texts and innumerable articles dealing with psychology and related fields. His devotion and depth and breadth of knowledge have provided leadership and inspiration in the training of psychologists who have gone on to help our youth in educational settings. The "right to read" is a current concern among educators and parents. The child who has trouble acquiring this essential skill has a difficult time adjusting to both school and society. I am grateful for the insights gained under Father Murray's direction at St. John's University, which enabled me to further develop techniques that can help an ever greater number of students to achieve literacy.

ACKNOWLEDGEMENTS

This book owes much to the people who have inspired and helped us — the children who in the process of being taught provided us with the opportunity to test our ideas; the participants in our workshop who pointed out the need for this instructional material; Mitchel Siegel, Art Director of the Ossining Public Schools, for his art work; Jean Goodman, Chairman of the English Department of the Ossining High School, for the Affix Chain; Barbara Lynds, Sue MacDonald, Gay Oden, and Carolyn Smith, coordinators of the Ossining Public Schools tutorial program, for help in producing this revised edition; Lillian and Murray Nanes for their assistance; and Bill and Anne for their patience.

Copyright © 1972, 1973, 1975, 1977 Educators Publishing Service, Inc.

First published in the United States of America in 1977 by the Walker Publishing Company, Inc.

Published simultaneously in Canada by Fitzhenry & Whiteside, Limited, Toronto

ISBN: 0-8027-9043-7

Library of Congress Catalog Card Number: 76-52275

Printed in the United States of America

10 9 8 7 6 5 4 3 2 1

PREFACE

A Recipe for Reading, like all good recipes, requires that you:

    1 — know what ingredients are needed,

    2 — understand how they are to be combined,
                   and

    3 — are able to adapt the recipe to individual needs.

This manual should be read in its entirety before being put to use. If the Recipe is followed with a dash of imagination and creativity, the results will be rewarding.

In this book, a letter in parentheses represents the letter's sound — (ă) is the short a sound, (ā) is the long a sound, for example. Other pronunciation symbols are based on Webster's Third International Dictionary.

PREFACE TO THE SECOND EDITION

This book fills a long felt need for a logically organized and successfully tested program of reading instruction. After years of teaching children, teachers, and tutors, I recorded my methods in the manual, Recipe for Reading.

From my background as a mathematician, I tried to put some predictable, logical order into the study of the written form of the language. Thus, the book contains clearly described sequential lesson plans. It indicates the way in which letters and their sounds are introduced for both writing and reading.

Instead of learning all the twenty-six lower and twenty-six upper case letters of the alphabet — fifty-two abstract symbols in all — only lower case letters are introduced. We start with seven consonants and two short vowels. These are used as a meaningful code in writing and reading phonetic words, phrases, and sentences. This is followed by the unique experience of reading one's first book!

The writer believes that children should read short books to have a sense of achievement. There are over a hundred such books listed to be read at appropriate stages in the sequence. They represent thirteen publishers and numerous authors and artists.

Emphasis is placed throughout on the positive approach to teaching. Thus the author's feeling is that as we teach, we remain keenly aware that life takes its course, happy at times, miserable at others, but filled with a deep mystery, with the promise of an unknown future and the drama of a hidden past.

Every person is a mystery that must be learned slowly, reverently, with care, tenderness, and pain, but is never learned completely.

Our philosophy is based on the belief that within us all there is at work a principle of growth to some good end and life-giving exuberance.

It is with great satisfaction that I state that teachers, tutors, and parents across the country have used this technique and have found it to be eminently successful, both as a basic text for classroom instruction and for "learning-disabled" children. In fact, when it has been used as a classroom technique, remarkably few children later needed supplementary remedial help.

NINA TRAUB

Ossining, New York
January 1977

CONTENTS

CHAPTER I
READING — A NATIONAL CONCERN   1

CHAPTER II
PREREQUISITES FOR SUCCESS   6

CHAPTER III
THE TECHNIQUE   10

CHAPTER IV
THE METHOD   14

CHAPTER V
CONSONANT-VOWEL-CONSONANT
WORDS AND SYLLABLES   25

CHAPTER VI
INTRODUCING TWO-SYLLABLE WORDS   70
    CONSONANT BLENDS   73
    "MAGIC E"   84

CHAPTER VII
INTRODUCING VOWEL DIGRAPHS   94
    SYLLABLE DIVISION   109
    HARD-SOFT C   136
    HARD-SOFT G   139

CHAPTER VIII
VOWEL-CONSONANT-VOWEL
SPELLING RULE   160
    ALTERNATE PRONUNCIATIONS   177
    AFFIXES AND ROOT WORDS   191
    SPELLING WITH AFFIXES   203

APPENDIX
INDEX TO PHONETIC READERS   207

BIBLIOGRAPHY   215

INDEX   216

Sequence Chart

	page
*c (hard as in cat)	26
*o (olive)	27
*a (apple)	28
*d	29
*g (hard as in go)	30
*m	31
*l	32
*h	33
*t	34
*i (Indian)	38
*j	39
*k	40
*p	41
*ch (chin)	42
*u (up)	43
*b	44
*r	46
*f	47
*n	48
*e (egg)	49
*s (sit)	51
*sh	52
*th (hard as in that)	53
*w	54
*wh	55
*y (yes)	56
*v	57
*x	58
*z	59
*th (soft as in thin)	60
*qu (queen)	61
Review Tests — CVC Words	63
Two-Syllable Compound Words	64
Spelling Rule — ff-ll-ss	65
Detached Syllables	67
Review Test — Detached Syllables — CVC	69
Introducing Two-Syllable Words	70
*Introducing Consonant Blends	73
Review Tests — Consonant Blends	76
Detached Syllables — Blends	77
Review Test — Detached Syllables — Blends	78
Two-Syllable Words with Blends	79
*Endings — ing-ang-ong-ung-ink-ank-onk-unk	80
*Magic e (i-e, o-e, u-e, a-e, e-e)	84
Review Test — Magic e	89
Detached Syllable — Magic e	91
Two-Syllable Words with Magic e	92
*ph (phone)	93
*ea (eat)	98
*oa (soap)	100
*ai (mail)	102
*ee (tree)	104

	page
*ay (play)	106
*oe (toe)	107
Syllable Division	109
Review Tests — Two Syllable Words	112
*er (her)	113
*ir (bird)	115
*ur (burn)	117
*ow (clown)	119
*ou (ouch)	121
*igh (light)	123
*Endings: ble-fle-tle-dle-gle-kle-ple-zle	124
*ild-old-ind-ost-olt Words	126
*ar (star)	127
*or (horn)	129
*oo (zoo)	130
*Endings: ly-vy-by-dy-ty-fy-ny-py-sy	131
*ck (black)	134
Hard-Soft c	136
Hard-Soft g	139
*ge-dge	142
Review Test — Hard-Soft c and g	143
*y as a Vowel	144
Use of Long Vowel in Syllable Division	145
*aw (straw)	149
*au (August)	151
*a (ball)	152
*oi (oil)	153
*oy (boy)	155
*tch (catch)	156
*ing as an Ending	158
VCV Spelling Rule	160
*Suffix - ed	166
*ew (grew)	168
*eigh (eight)	169
*ie (chief)	170
*eu (Europe)	171
*ei (ceiling)	172
*tion (action)	173
*ue (rescue)	175
*sion (division)	176
*ow (snow)	178
*ch (school)	179
*ea (head)	180
*oo (good)	181
*ew (few)	182
*ei (vein)	183
*ue (true)	184
*ou (group)	185
*sion (mansion)	186
*ea (great)	188
*ch (machine)	189
*s (is)	190
Affixes and Root Words	191
Spelling with Affixes	203

CHAPTER I

READING—A NATIONAL CONCERN

Eight million children in America's elementary and secondary schools today will not learn to read adequately. One child in seven is handicapped in his ability to acquire essential reading skills. This phenomenon pervades all segments of our society— black and white, boys and girls, the poor and the affluent.[1]

The study of reading disabilities in the United States made by the Secretary's (HEW) National Advisory Committee on Dyslexia and Related Disorders addresses its attention primarily to "the problems manifested by those individuals who, in spite of apparently adequate intelligence and emotional stability, exhibit difficulties in learning to read within a teaching program that proves effective for most children."[2] This study indicates that:

Approximately 15 percent of the total school population conforms to this description. This number could certainly be reduced by the improvement of regular classroom instruction. But a majority of these children, in order to overcome their handicaps and complete a normal educational experience, need remedial assistance.[3]

The committee further states that "early identification of such students and special intervention in their training may be necessary if they are to overcome their difficulties and become capable of satisfactory achievement."[4] However, the report points out that the problem is accentuated because of the lack of adequately trained personnel.

An important observation in the report is that the program should be directed to the "prevention of reading failure through the improvement of beginning reading instruction and towards help for the child who is already failing."[5] Furthermore, the Commission realizes the need for developing diagnostic tech-

---

[1] Report of the Secretary's (HEW) National Advisory Committee on Dyslexia and Related Disorders, Reading Disorders in the United States (August 1969), p. 4.

[2] Ibid., p. 6

[3] Idem.

[4] Ibid., p. 8.

[5] Ibid., p. 47.

niques which would identify the nature of the problem, and it suggests that more work is needed to provide methods for overcoming the handicap.

To date, more than twenty thousand professional papers have been published on learning disabilities and the need for corrective action. This mass of literature reflects the growing awareness of the widespread nature of this syndrome. Work in the field by educators, pediatricians, neurologists, psychologists, ophthalmologists, and optometrists confirm the need for a concerted effort to assist these students.

Reading — A Complex Task

No two people are neurologically the same and no one is neurologically perfect. Neurological idiosyncrasies make each of us unique. R.M.N. Crosby, a pediatric neurologist and neurosurgeon, writes that:

> Reading is the most complex neurological task a person undertakes in his lifetime. That human beings are able to read at all is a miracle. Yet, most of us are able to do it so effortlessly that we fail to realize how difficult it is.[6]

Reading requires visual perception and discrimination, visual memory and recall, and directional orientation. In addition, visual-auditory integration is needed to translate visual symbols into meaningful auditory equivalents. These include the synthesis of letter-sounds into syllables and syllables into words. A still higher level of integration is required for reading comprehension. However, millions learn to read due to the diligence and persistence of student and teacher.

The child with learning disabilities needs special techniques. We find that the whole-word or look-and-say method is a disaster for a child with impaired visual perception. A phonic approach may be less effective for a child with auditory imperception and, likewise, the kinesthetic method might not work for the child who has poor tactile perception. Each student must be separately diagnosed and a plan of remedial therapy developed. At present, except for a few fortunate individuals, disabled readers do not receive the benefit of precise diagnosis or of carefully planned individualized instruction as do other handicapped youngsters.

Answering a Need

Twenty years ago, when I was a certified teacher tutoring in my community, the principal of the local elementary school called to say that they had given up hope for a fourth grade boy. He asked me to see what I could do for Sandy, a very nervous boy who was unable to read, spell, write or do arithmetic. I used every approach I could think of without noticeable success.

---

[6]R.M.N. Crosby and Robert Liston, The Waysiders (New York: Delacorte Press, 1968), p. 51.

I sent Sandy to a pediatrician to check out possible physiological causes of his disability. The doctor reported that, although he displayed extreme nervousness due to environmental stress, his vision and hearing were normal and he was in good physical condition. The doctor recommended psychological testing and a thorough investigation by Dr. Paul Dozier, a neuropsychiatrist. Dr. Dozier informed us that Sandy had a severe case of specific learning disability, but he assured us that he had normal intelligence and *COULD BE TAUGHT*.

A tutor was needed who had been trained to teach children with learning disabilities. Since none were available, I was asked if I would be willing to learn the necessary remedial techniques. Under the supervision of Dr. Dozier I acquired the skills from Anna Gillingham, who for two years had been a research associate with the neurologist Dr. Samuel T. Orton at the Neurological Institute in New York. As a result of their collaboration, effective techniques for teaching children with specific learning disabilities had been developed. With their guidance I was able to teach Sandy to read. In time, he went on to and graduated from college and is now a responsible and happily married man.

Since then I have continued my interest in further developing techniques which would help other students like Sandy. Over the past twenty years I have helped hundreds of these children by continuously developing and testing techniques that have been organized to form the contents of this manual. Dr. Crosby writes that:

> The vast majority of normal children will learn to read despite the methods of instruction used. It logically follows that, if ideal teaching methods are used, the same child may learn more easily and at an earlier age. More importantly, the minority of children who are dyslexic may be helped over this necessary educational hurdle.[7]

Signs of Learning Disabilities

Every teacher should be trained to be alert to signs that might suggest a specific disability. The following is a quick checklist to use when one finds a child who, although he has normal vision, hearing, and intelligence, has difficulty keeping up with the class in the language skills.

1. Disturbances in speech are common if learning to talk began late—at ages three or four—and words were and continue to be mispronounced.

2. Note the following aspects.
   a) Left-handedness

---

[7]Crosby, Op. cit., p: 66.

b) Alternation in lateral dominance

c) Significant defects in left-right discrimination

3. Dysgraphia (poor handwriting) is present. The student is better at copying than at spontaneous writing. Reversals are observed in various performances—confusion of reversible letter, the "static reversals," and letter-order errors. He can more easily than others mirror read and write—the "kinetic reversals."

4. The child is poor in written work but participates with intelligent oral questions and responses.

5. A striking finding is that nonphonetic words in this child's limited sight vocabulary are often written incorrectly, whereas a perfectly phonetic word, even when it is totally unfamiliar, may be written correctly. In fact, he can often spell better than he can read or vice-versa.

6. Difficulty in figure-ground perception is present.

7. Difficulty in comprehending written language exists.

8. Reading is avoided, but information is sought. He derives pleasure in a normal way from listening to stories and participates in discussion and conversation.

9. Unusual interest in drawing and mechanics is apparent.

10. He is restless, hyperactive and easily distractible.

11. He is hypokinetic (sluggish).

12. He may be unusually clumsy.

13. Emotional disturbances are usually present due to the child's failure in one or more of the following—spelling, writing, arithmetic or reading.

14. The familial incidence of this problem is impressive. It is a dominant trait.

15. One should check to see if the child can read the words in the reader out of context as frequently as possible at the first grade level. The textbook can easily be memorized and, thus, the problem can be overlooked.

16. Boys are afflicted about four times as often as girls.

One or more of the above symptoms associated with difficulties in academic learning should prompt the teacher to seek a psychological evaluation. Ideally, the diagnosis of the problem should be made no later than the middle of the first grade.

Some characteristic emotional disorders tend to be mistakenly interpreted as the <u>primary</u> or <u>fundamental</u> cause of the child's inability to read rather than <u>secondary</u> and <u>reactive</u> to it. Yet, reading disability is one of the most common and least recognized causes of school failure. It is a significant factor underlying school behavioral problems, dropouts and the drift to juvenile delinquency. We no longer use the hickory stick, but, somewhere from the first grade on, the child with learning disabilities has begun to hurt. For him, the atmosphere for learning is a punitive experience.

1. He gets low grades.

2. He is placed in the slow group.

3. He disappoints parents and teachers.

4. He incurs the ridicule of classmates in his academic endeavors, in gym and on the playground.

5. He fails a grade.

6. <u>And he himself is the most disappointed of all!</u>

CHAPTER II

PREREQUISITES FOR SUCCESS

The objective of this manual is to facilitate the teachings of reading to all children, including those children with learning disabilities who, up to this time, have been unable to fit into the mainstream of the regular educational classroom. The manual will serve as a guide for presenting the work in carefully planned stages, so as to protect students from a sense of bewilderment or failure. To accommodate variable learning rates, Sequence Charts have been designed to help teachers record the individual progress of each child. A sample chart is printed on page vi.

The manual, which represents more than one year of classwork, should be read in its entirety before being put to use. The concepts are based on successful teaching experience, but it is expected that teacher initiative and creative ability will supplement the basic presentation.

Reading Skill Development

Talking is language—reading is language. Most first graders have already acquired a knowledge and use of the spoken language in response to auditory stimuli. They learned to talk by hearing others talk. The visual stimulus of abstract symbols, however, is the challenge that must be faced in order to acquire necessary skills for mastering the written language.

In the early stages of learning these skills, a child's vocabulary is so limited that the reading matter tends to be uninteresting. At this time, stories are read at the child's interest level with the attention given to acquiring comprehension skills through discussion. These discussions should be geared to developing the capacity for organization, inference, judgment and imagery. However, we must not assume that a child is able to picture words and concepts that are completely outside of his experience. A child who has lived all his life in an apartment house would have difficulty knowing what an attic is. Thus, we must rely on the child's curiosity to hold his interest when we read to him, but we must be careful not to go beyond his capacity to comprehend.

If basic phonic skills are carefully developed, the child will encounter less difficulty with more complex application. Therefore, care should be taken to pace instruction to the needs of the child rather than to the rapid completion of material. This approach is designed to give the student a feeling of success every step of the way.

When a sufficiently large reading vocabulary has been acquired, begin to work on comprehension skills in the material the child is reading himself. This should be done in the form of oral discussion until he is quite comfortable with the mechanics of writing and spelling. Do not hold back the creativity of the child by asking him to slowly and laboriously write only those things that he can spell. Instead, encourage him to dictate stories which can be typed into books.

An Atmosphere for Learning

It is advisable to have all reading, writing, and spelling lessons held at the same time and place each day. To minimize distractions, the room should appear orderly and uncluttered. It should be well-lighted and ventilated. The children should all be facing the same direction when working with the written language. This helps orient them in space and, especially, in the awareness of left-right directionality.

To help establish the above, it is suggested that you place a large poster of a bat and ball with a <u>b</u> below it on the right wall. On the left wall place another poster of a drum and drumstick with a <u>d</u> below it. The use of permanent fixtures in the room can further reinforce directionality. For example, one can say, "The circle of the <u>d</u> turns to the window and the circle of the <u>b</u> turns to the blackboard." Once a cue has been established, it should be consistently referred to and <u>not changed</u>. A predictable daily routine will create a state of mind conducive to learning.

Instructor's Role

Interaction of instructor and student must be directed to establishing an optimal learning atmosphere for the child. All statements to the child, comments on his work and directions are given in the <u>positive form</u>. One should avoid negative comments as they tend to undermine the confidence of the student. Examples of deleterious remarks and their alternatives follow:

Avoid These	Use These Instead
"What did you do that for?"	"This is the way to do it."
"Don't you know any better?"	"Let me help you."
"I've told you and told you, but you still do it."	"Here is another way of doing it."
"If you would only listen and pay attention!"	"Listen."
"Just try a little harder and you'll get it right."	"Let's try it this way."
"You've made a mistake."	"Make this change and it will be right."
"You have five words wrong."	"You have fifteen correct."

Criticism often results in disruptive classroom behavior and causes a negative attitude toward further learning. "Laziness," "not paying attention," and "not trying" are not diagnostic terms. The teacher must go back to a point where a child can successfully handle the task, carefully analyze the component elements of the item that stumps him, and, by small increments, lead him to success.

On a spelling list, do not cross out or write over in red ink when boat is spelled bote. The pencilled bote with the red-inked boat superimposed on it is a confusing visual stimulus. Say instead, "The ($\bar{o}$) sound in this word has the oa spelling." Put the appropriate phonic card in front of him and tell him, "You have the beginning two letters right." Have the incorrect part of the word erased and have him rewrite it correctly. Thus, he has the proper visual image before him and a paper that is not "bleeding."

We have occasionally heard teachers say, "How often have I told you to put your name on the left side of the paper and the date on the right? If you would only pay attention, I would not have to keep telling you again and again." She may not realize that some children confuse left and right and will not consistently perform this task correctly. Because we want to protect the child from reinforcing his error through practice, next time, <u>before</u> he puts the heading on the paper, say, "Write your name on the left side of the paper which is the side near the window."

Be certain that the directions for all lessons are brief and to the point. The child cannot sort immense quantities of words. He must be guided by precise, well-organized instructions. I have often used this analogy in lecturing to teachers. "When giving directions to a friend on how to reach a destination, you would tell him where to make the <u>correct</u> turns rather than confusing him and weighing him down with the many turns along the road which he should <u>not</u> take."

To sum up, there are many ingredients that go into creating an optimal learning situation for children. Successful teaching of reading is based first upon the teacher's awareness of the needs and basic capacities of her students. Then, her attention must be focused on "how and what to do."

CHAPTER III

THE TECHNIQUE

Our written language is composed of abstract symbols combined to make meaningful words. It is when a student is introduced to the abstract visual stimulus of the written language that he may encounter difficulties. To make these abstract symbols meaningful and workable, we begin by introducing only nine carefully selected letters. The sequence in which sounds are introduced throughout this book has been chosen because some letters and sounds are more easily written and learned than others. Sequence is determined by auditory, visual and kinesthetic factors rather than by alphabetical order. In the first nine letters, c, o, a, d and g have the same kinesthetic formation and are made by turning the circle to the left. Hard c and g seem to be among the easiest sounds perceived by the ear. D and m are among the first sounds formed by the infant—"da-da," "ma-ma." However, d and b are introduced at a considerable distance from each other, because they are the pair that are most commonly reversed and confused.

These nine letters are used to form words for spelling and reading, sentences for dictation and reading, and story books for reading. As each additional letter is added to the original nine, the child's spelling and reading vocabulary grows.

With each letter we give the appropriate visual, auditory and kinesthetic factors that are utilized. By that we mean, carefully teaching the letter as seen by the child and heard by the child and felt by the child in speaking its sound and forming its proper shape in writing.

Auditory

Many of the letters will have suggestions for associating symbol to sound. In addition, the teacher's enunciation must be clear and accurate and she must be particularly careful not to add vowels to the consonant sounds.

Kinesthetic

The proper kinesthetic formation of the letter is emphasized with a dot to represent the point at which the pencil is placed on the paper to start the letter and arrows to designate the direction. At the top of each page in the left- and right-hand corner, respectively, we have a "drum and stick" and a "bat and ball." These are suggested directional aids for the child who reverses symbols or forms letters incorrectly.

Writing (Figure-Ground)

The letters of our English language have four points of orientation to facilitate the decoding of the symbols used. Consider the symbol $\mathscr{O}$. It is p̲, b̲, d̲ or q̲ depending entirely upon its position in space. To orient the child, we use a specially lined paper for writing.* We draw two blue parallel lines and two red parallel lines between them.

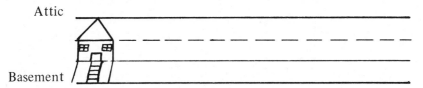

For the younger child, we call the red parallel lines the "little red house." This is a concrete rather than an abstract concept which helps him to recognize the limits that these lines create. The blue line above is called the "attic" and the one below is called the "basement." It is necessary that the child know the meaning of these terms. If he does not, they should be modified to "upstairs" and "downstairs" or whatever else is meaningful. The verbalization accompanying the writing of the letter will help him to form it correctly.

For example: P̲ starts in the "little red house," runs down to the "basement," up the stairs again, and the big, fat tummy turns to the "bat and ball."

In this way, the symbol is completely determined in space.

The student learns how to write a letter by first tracing a model and then writing it independently. It is important to teach that the pencil should not be lifted from the paper until the letter is completed. This reinforces the proper kinesthetic formation and carries over into cursive writing.

All writing should be done in pencil with an attached eraser, never a pen. Should there be an error in writing or spelling, never say "This is wrong." Have the child erase the item you want modified, repeat the word clearly again and help him make his own correction.

Introducing Additional Sounds

After the first nine letters (c, o, a, d, g, m, l, h, t) are taught and the child has learned to use them in writing, spelling and reading, the subsequent sounds are introduced in sequence one at a time. The new material is presented at the beginning of the lesson, after the drill. The card with the new sound is clearly displayed in front of the child while it is being taught. He learns to write and spell a word before he attempts to read it.

*Spirit Duplicating Masters for this paper may be obtained from Educators Publishing Service, Inc., 75 Moulton Street, Cambridge, Massachusetts 02138.

It is necessary to follow the recommended sequence as shown inside the front cover, since each group of words and sentences utilizes only the sounds taught up to that point. A separate set of these sound cards should be provided and kept for each student.

Some of the suggestions given for introducing a sound may seem elaborate and dramatic. This is deliberate in order to impress upon the child's mind a meaningful association with the abstract symbol. It is particularly helpful to a young child or to one who is having learning difficulties. Yet, it is by no means the only way of introducing a sound. Supplementary methods of presentation are left to the teacher's ingenuity.

In a classroom the children respond in unison, but the teacher must, at regular intervals, see each child individually to make sure there are no gaps in his knowledge.

The student's progress must be carefully documented. All of his work is dated and kept in a folder. This gives him a sense of value for what he has produced and an indication of the teacher's respect for his effort. He and his family can see evidence of his progress. A sheet is kept in front of the folder where the growing count of words is kept. For example, the first set consists of thirty-three words. Let us say, in a subsequent lesson, a child learns six additional words. The word count then becomes thirty-nine. It is amazing how much pleasure and satisfaction the child derives from seeing his word count grow. A sheet on which he keeps a record of the books he has read is entitled "Bibliography" and is also placed in the front part of the folder.

The younger child is always given some sign of approval on his paper such as a rubber stamp, a decal or a star. The teacher ends the lesson with work in which the child has acquired competence. This can be in the form of review or word games. Thus the child concludes his lesson with an awareness of the progress he is making. Incorporating the insights of the behavioral scientists, we can, in a small group or in a one-to-one situation, have a "treasure chest" from which he can select a small piece of candy at the end of the lesson.

An Approach for Older Children

A reading program for the older student should follow the same developmental sequence we have presented so far. Whether his problem is spelling and/or reading, exposure to a structured phonic base will help him develop skills in word analysis. He may move through the beginning sounds and rules very quickly. However, when an area is discovered in which he is weak or confused, it should be clarified and drilled until it is understood. It is helpful to show him how to break down multisyllabic words into simple syllables that are easier to decode for spelling and reading.

The following explanation of the program is suggested to help him accept what appears to be humiliatingly simple material: "You have had difficulty in the past with your reading and/or spelling. We will help you break the barrier by teaching you the code. For instance, think of a spy who gets a message by radio in Morse code.

'The radioman listens to the sound of the dots and dashes and translates them into letters which he writes on a piece of paper. But when he finishes taking the entire message, he cannot understand the message because it has been sent in cryptographic code. The message was just a jumble of letters and numbers that had no meaning to him. . . The radioman takes the message to the intelligence officer who gets out his code book and translates the message into understandable English and takes the appropriate action.'[8]

"Our alphabet is a code. It is, however, an imperfect code since one sound may have many symbols and one symbol may stand for more than one sound. The English language has forty-five basic sounds with only twenty-six letters of the alphabet representing them; seventy common phonograms have been developed to represent our written language.

"We will teach you how to intelligently decode the written English language. We could do this by training you on long unfamiliar words, but it can be done much faster if we start with three-letter words. Master the use of these twenty-six symbols and you are well on your way to decoding words."

---

[8]Crosby, Op. cit., p. 42.

CHAPTER IV

THE METHOD

Required Materials

1. Phonetic sound cards . Use 3" x 5" unlined index cards to make a set of phonetic sound cards. Print one asterisked (*) item from the Sequence Chart (see page vi) on each card.

    Magic markers are best for this purpose. Use red for vowels and vowel digraphs and black for consonants.

2. Phonetic word cards . The phonetic words that are listed for each sound should be printed with a black magic marker on 3" x 5" unlined index cards — one word to a card.

3. Phonetic phrase cards . The phonetic phrases that are listed for each sound should be printed with a black magic marker on 5" x 8" unlined index cards — one sentence to a card. At this point, a 4" x 6" unlined index card and a primer typewriter may also be used.

4. Phonetic sentence cards . The phonetic sentences that are listed for each sound should be printed with a black magic marker on 5" x 8" unlined index cards — one sentence to a card. At this point, a 4" x 6" unlined index card and a primer typewriter may also be used.

5. Phonetic story books . Phonetic story books from Alphabet Series I should be used where indicated in the text. The publisher of these and other phonetic readers are listed on page 21.

6. Phonetic word games . A large variety of drill games, using phonetic words at the appropriate sequence level, provide an interesting and pleasant way to reinforce skills. For suggestions, see O'Neal and Zylstra, Independent Creative Ideas for Use with Specific Language Disability Children, available from Educators Publishing Service, Inc. — see page 21. Other sources are the Dolch Teaching Aids (Garrard Publishing Co., 1607 No. Market St., Champaign, Ill. 61820 and the Kenworthy Educational Service, Buffalo, N. Y.).

7. Sequence charts . A teacher should record the progress and current position in the sequence on the child's individual sequence chart (see page vi). This will serve as a valuable record for the teacher as well as a convenient way to communicate the child's progress to others — e.g., teachers, parents, psychologists.

8. Writing paper . Have the student write his name on an unlined piece of paper. Then select the size which will provide the best fit to his spontaneous writing. See page 11.

14

To aid in organizing the above required materials, <u>use a file box with dividers</u>. The first divider will have the introductory group of nine letters (<u>c</u>, <u>o</u>, <u>a</u>, <u>d</u>, <u>g</u>, <u>m</u>, l, <u>h</u>, <u>t</u>) listed on it. The divider is followed by the corresponding phonetic sound cards, 34 phonetic word cards (see page 35), 4 phonetic phrase cards (see page 36) and 7 phonetic sentence cards (page 36). The second divider will have the letter *i* on it, and is followed by a phonetic sound card (i), 11 phonetic word cards, 4 phonetic phrase cards and 5 phonetic sentence cards (page 38). Continue in like manner throughout the sequence of additional sounds, making an individual divider for each new sound.

Presenting the Lesson

The lesson should start with a daily drill of the phonetic sound cards. This serves as a tuning up process. The routine can be compared to the practicing of scales or tuning up prior to playing a musical instrument. As this skill is perfected, it will take only a few minutes at the beginning of each lesson.

1. **The teacher flashes all of the <u>phonic sound cards</u> that have been learned. The child responds to each with the proper sound.**

   Should the student fail to respond correctly, have him trace the letter in the proper kinesthetic fashion while the teacher is making the sound and giving him the proper associative clue. Have him imitate the sound.

   The larger the teacher makes the letter, the easier it will be to deal with it as a visual stimulus. The larger the student writes the letter, the better he can relate it to the configuration visually and kinesthetically. In extreme cases, associate a three-dimensional object with each letter in addition to associating with sensations in his own body. This is described subsequently in the manual as each letter is introduced.

2. **The teacher makes the <u>sound of each letter</u> learned so far. The child responds to each by <u>naming it</u> and <u>writing it</u>.**

   The correct kinesthetic formation of the letter is mandatory. The student learns how to write a letter by <u>first tracing a model and then writing it independently</u>. It is important to teach that the pencil should not be lifted from the paper until the letter is completed. This reinforces the proper kinesthetic formation and carries over into cursive writing.

   When the child does not respond correctly to the auditory stimulus of the sound of the letter given by the teacher, <u>she traces a large letter with two fingers on his lower back</u>, saying, "This says (ă) and the name of the letter is <u>a</u>." The child then writes the letter, giving its name as he does it.

In cases of difficulty with letter formation, try any of the following:

1) A large letter is formed with masking tape on the floor, and the child walks it.

2) The child forms a large letter on the floor with heavy rope and walks it in the proper kinesthetic fashion with his shoes off or barefoot.

3) Plasticene or clay may be rolled into a string and shaped into the form of the letter, first by the teacher and then by the student. He then traces the letter with eyes open and with eyes shut.

4) He traces a large letter written on sandpaper or cut out of sandpaper.

5) He writes the letter with his finger on the desk top.

6) He writes the letter on a tray filled with sand, salt, sugar, chocolate sauce or icing with his two fingers (the index and the middle finger).

7) He writes the letter in the air.

8) He makes the letter with finger paints.

9) He dips a small sponge in paint and makes a large letter on newspaper or newsprint.

3. **New material, if any, is presented after the drills. The student is taught to write and spell the words in the new lesson before he is taught to read them. The teacher dictates a word. The child repeats the word and spells it out loud before he writes it and again while writing it.**

When the nine sounds (c, o, a, d, g, m, l, h, t) have been learned the child is shown how they are formed into words. He is told that, since he knows the sounds of all these letters, he will have no problem in using them in spelling and reading. The teacher says, "I am going to give you X words that you will be able to spell without having to study them first."

Should he have difficulty in spelling the word, tell him to listen for the first sound only. Say, "b-b-bat." When he tells you that the first letter is b, tell him to write it. Then have him listen for the vowel and say, "ba-a-at." He will name the vowel and then write it. In like manner, have him listen for the last sound, "ba-t-t-t." He will name it and write it. As the child's auditory discrimination improves, dictate the words in a more natural manner. Discuss the meaning of any word unfamiliar to the child.

We shall make a practice of giving the definitions of the more unusual words. Children enjoy acquiring this skill. Note the pleasure in quoting Mary Poppins' "supercalifragilisticexpealidocious."

4. In the <u>reading and blending of sounds</u>, the child reads all the words he has spelled from the phonetic word cards, not from his own paper.

If the child has difficulty reading the word on the card, put the three sound cards of which the word is composed in the appropriate sequence below it. Have him give each sound, first from the individual cards and then from the word card. Should there still be difficulty in blending, try any of the following:

1) Have him sound the letters on the first card, slide the next one to touch it, at which point he begins to sound the second. In like manner, add the third sound.

2) For the child who cannot blend three-letter words, have him start by blending the initial two letters, that is, the consonant and the vowel that follows it. Then add the final consonant. It is also possible to make families of the same initial two sounds, to which are added different final consonants. In this way the left-right orientation is consistently maintained.

For example:

ma - mad	ha - had	co - cod
ma - mat	ha - ham	co - cog
	ha - hat	co - cot
	ha - hag	

We prefer this to the common practice of teaching blending as in the "<u>at</u> family."

at - bat - fat - hat - etc.

Reading the end of the word first adds to the left-right sequencing confusion.

3) Have the child sing the sounds in sequence in a low tone.

4) Tell him that the sounds "stick" together.

5) Tell him to give the sounds quickly.

6) Tell him that the first letter is the locomotive and it pulls the others along.

7) Have the child hold a rubber band or rolled spring tape measure. Pull it out slowly as you make the three sounds. Tell child to s-t-r-e-t-ch the sounds. Then let go to snap, making the rubber band (or tape measure) word short. That's blending. (Courtesy of Sister Mary Consilia, Mt. St. Mary, Newburgh, N.Y.)

8) Use a pen flashlight to focus on each letter in a word and slide the light across word to blend.

9) In severe cases put a green, yellow and red dot above each of the three letters. Say "When the light is green you go, yellow — slow down, and red — stop."

10) Point with pencil eraser above the word, one letter at a time, from left to right.

11) Use magnetic lowercase letters (available from Playskool Inc.) and slide them together to blend into a word.

12) Should the student have difficulty with vowels as well as blending, we do the following:

a) Place the card with o on the desk and dictate the following sounds.

   hŏ - dŏ - cŏ - gŏ - mŏ - lŏ - tŏ

   Print each of the above on individual cards and have the student read them.

b) Place the card with a on the desk and dictate the following sounds.

   dă - tă - mă - lă - că - hă

   Print each of the above on individual cards and have the student read them.

c) Have the child add a third letter to his o family as you dictate at random.

   do - hot - mom - cod - lot - Tod

d) Have the child read cards with the three-letter words on them.

e) To be sure he can comfortably handle vowel discrimination, mix the two groups of two-letter cards for spelling and reading. If he cannot do this readily, go back to the original drill.

18

f) When the above is mastered, mix the two groups of three-letter words for spelling and reading.

5. **When using <u>sentences for dictation and reading</u>, the teacher dictates one or more sentences, depending upon the ease with which the child writes. The child repeats the sentences and spells each word out loud as he writes it.**

Sentences for Dictation

A student can often spell words in a spelling list but fails to write them correctly in a sentence. Thus, the sentences that follow each new sound function as the review of spelling and reading. We start with short sentences and gradually increase their length. If he cannot cope with a full sentence, dictate a phrase at a time.

In dictating, any nonphonetic word is placed on a card in front of the student for copying. These words are shown underlined in the sentences beginning on page 36. The teacher points to it when she comes to it in dictation. Our object is never to "catch" a child in error or to confuse him, but to clearly show him how he can apply the principles he is learning easily and successfully.

Memory Training

The following technique is helpful in assisting those students who, during dictation, forget what the sentence is. The child is given a word orally and is told to carry it in his mind to some point in the room and to come back with it. For example, the teacher points to the vase on her desk and says, "vase." The child goes to the back of the room, touches the wall, comes back to the teacher, and says, "vase." Then she says, "What else can you say about the vase?" He may say, "yellow." He takes "yellow vase" in his mind, walks to the door, comes back and says to the teacher, "yellow vase." This is expanded to "yellow vase on the desk," etc., until the sentence becomes too long for the child to repeat verbatim to the teacher. For the student who cannot think of descriptive words, the teacher, at least in the beginning, should offer suggestions.

6. **The child <u>reads the sentences</u> he has written <u>from the cards</u>, not from his own paper.**

1) The nonphonetic word is underlined to indicate that the student is not responsible for it. The sentence should first be read silently. Allow him to point with his finger or to use a marker. This helps him to separate figure from ground and protects him from losing his place.

19

2) The student should ask for help if he is not sure of a word. The teacher helps him <u>to decode it</u> but does not give him the word.

3) The sentence must then be read smoothly when it is read out loud.

    a) Tell him to read "as though he were talking."

    b) Have him make believe he is a TV announcer.

    c) For a child who mumbles or reads in a low voice, as is frequently the case with unsure readers, have him make believe he is on the stage and the people in the back row want to hear him.

7. **The child reads <u>phonetic storybooks</u>**. Use the Alphabet Series I, <u>Recipe for Reading</u> sequence and <u>appropriate</u> books from other publishers.

Use the same techniques as described for reading sentences. He may progress to preparing two or more sentences at a time and then to a paragraph at a time.

Alternate Oral Reading

The teacher and child take turns reading alternate sentences in a story. This progresses to two sentences at a time and then to a paragraph at a time. Two-character plays lend themselves particularly well to this method.

Alternate reading gives the child a model by which he can read smoothly and with expression. It is a friendly, shared activity and provides another opportunity to read for understanding and enjoyment. It helps if the teacher reacts with comments on the passage being read.

8. **The child plays <u>phonetic word games</u>.**

Games provide extra practice in a specific skill and replace plain drill. They have a high motivational value and provide more social interaction than most reading tasks. Repeated drill is often objected to as being monotonous. However, the same task presented in the form of a game is anticipated with pleasure. We have used them successfully at the end of a lesson so that the child leaves relaxed, with a sense of being competent in a skill and of having had fun.

As a new letter or sound is added to the child's repertoire of knowledge, the accompanying words are also added to the game.

Independent Reading

It is valuable to have a variety of books available for reinforcement of the reading skill. They help to promote an interest in reading and protect the child from monotony and memorization of the text. The first-grader has often escaped discovery as a non-reader, because he has memorized the text.

When financially possible, the children get a great deal of pleasure from being permitted to take home and to keep the book they have read. The series below are essentially phonetic in orientation and are recommended as supplementary books for the student's reading. Individual storybooks and series that complement the teaching sequence are listed in the Appendix.

PHONETIC READERS

1. Alphabet Series I
   Primary Phonics Storybooks
   A Phonetic Reader Series
   The Teaching Box Storybooks
   Educators Publishing Service, Inc.
   75 Moulton St.
   Cambridge, Mass. 02138

2. Palo Alto Reading Program
   Harcourt Brace & Jovanovich, Inc.
   757 Third Ave.
   New York, N.Y. 10017

3. Merrill Linguistic Readers
   Charles E. Merrill Publishing Co.
   1300 Alum Creek Dr.
   Columbus, Ohio 43216

4. Sullivan Programmed Reading
   Webster Division
   McGraw-Hill Book Co.
   Princeton Rd.
   Highstown, N.J. 08520

5. Open Court Basic Readers
   Open Court Publishing Co.
   1039 Eighth St.
   LaSalle, Ill. 61301

6. Miami Linguistic Series
   D.C. Heath and Co.
   125 Spring St.
   Lexington,
   Mass. 02173

7. S.R.A. Basic Reading Series
   Science Research Inc.
   259 East Erie St.
   Chicago, Ill. 60611
   (Levels A, B, C & D)

8. "Let's Read" Readers
   Clarence L. Barnhart
   Box 250
   Bronxville, N.Y. 10708
   (Bloomfield Readers)

9. Lippincott Basic Reading Series
   J.B. Lippincott Co.
   East Washington Sq.
   Philadelphia, Pa. 19105
   (*Reading Goals,* red book, blue book, orange book)

10. Fun Readers
    M.W. Sullivan Stories
    Behavioral Research Lab.
    Box 577
    Palo Alto, Cal. 94302

(continued)

11. Pacemaker Classics, Story Books,
True Adventures
Fearon Publishers, Educational Div.
6 Davis Dr.
Belmont, Cal. 94002

12. Structural Reading Series
Random House/Singer
School Div.
201 E. 50 St.
New York, N.Y. 10022

After the theory has been covered and applied to reading in phonetic books, the child is ready for books at his age and interest level. These are available in a form that can be handled by one who is reading below his grade level. We recommend that, when these books are introduced, they should start one year below his reading level.

Student Dictates Story

The child should be given the opportunity to dictate a story which is then typed on a primer typewriter or is printed by the teacher so that there is approximately one sentence at the bottom of each page. It is then made into a book for him. He is encouraged to illustrate the story with a drawing, cutouts, etc.

When the teacher prints the story, she may give the child an opportunity to practice writing by placing the printed story over a few carbons. The child then traces the letters with a pencil to produce carbon copies of his story. In addition to providing practice in writing, this gives him the satisfaction of having several copies of his book.

We find that a child can read a book composed of his own spontaneous vocabulary at a greater level of difficulty than the textbook material. This helps to develop verbal expression and the acquisition of a sight vocabulary.

Reading for Meaning

In the early stages of learning to read, the child's skills are insufficient for him to read interesting, exciting and meaningful material. At this time, it is important for an adult to read to the child at his interest level. This sparks an interest in reading. It also provides an opportunity for him to develop comprehension skills and to acquire information.

Listening for Meaning

The child can be read to for sheer pleasure or it can be an exercise in reading comprehension.

1. Ask the student to listen for the answer to a given question before you start reading the story. In the beginning, the answer is to be found in a specific paragraph. As his skill increases, the question is to be found in an increasingly longer selection.

2. As comprehension skills increase, he is given responsibility for two or more questions.

3. The selection is read and unanticipated questions are asked.

Reading at Home

Parents should be advised to take children to the library. They should read to them daily especially at bedtime after the "battle" to undress, wash up, clean teeth, etc., is over. They are to be encouraged to build bookshelves in the child's room or somewhere in the house. As often as possible, books should be bought as gifts.

To help develop an orientation in space, it is good to have a world map that covers a wall in the home. This can be referred to as stories are read.

They should be encouraged to watch "The Electric Company" on educational television stations.

SUMMARY OF DAILY ROUTINE

Every lesson should proceed as follows:

Teacher —   Pupil —

Teacher	Pupil
1. Shuffles and then flashes the phonic sound cards.	Gives the sound(s) he has learn-ed for the letter(s) on each card.
2. Reshuffles the pack. Gives the sound of each letter one at a time.	Names and writes as many spellings of the sound as he has been taught.*
3. If the child is ready, teaches a new sound and displays the letter in front of him.	Learns to make the new sound and uses proper kinesthetic formation of the letter when writing by: a) Tracing it. b) Copying it.
4. Dictates the words using the new letter.	Repeats the word, spells it orally and says each letter as he writes it.
5. Presents the above words on flash cards.	Reads the words he has spelled.
6. If *no* new sound has been taught —	child spells review words, child reads review words.
7. If time permits, dictates one or more sentences.	Repeats sentence, tries to remember it, spells out loud as he writes it.
8. Presents sentences on flash cards.	Reads the sentences.
9.	Reads a book at his appropriate level.
10. Teaches via phonetic word game.	

The lesson *MUST* end with work in which the child has acquired skill and ease in performance. That is, give him words, sentences, or books that are easy for him to read. He may play a card game consisting of words that no longer present any difficulty. The new words that he has learned are added to his word count and, if a book has been read, it is added to his "Bibliography" (see page 12). Finally, he can help himself to a gift from the "treasure chest" as he leaves.

*Alternatively, the teacher may give a key word which will tell the child which spelling is required.

24

CHAPTER V

CONSONANT–VOWEL–CONSONANT WORDS AND SYLLABLES

The sequence that follows will be a logical development of gradually expanding knowledge. It has been carefully structured so as to develop a feeling of accomplishment and success in the student. However, the creative teacher will be alert to the needs of the individual child and will adapt to the child's situation.

It is important that each child learn at his own rate. The length of a lesson depends upon age and concentration span. At the beginning, some children can sit and work productively at a desk for no more than five minutes at a time. As they progress, fifteen minutes a day of instruction can result in significant progress. The average child can work for one half-hour a day. The time span can be increased to one hour.

When we are beginning to teach a child who has <u>no</u> skills in the use of letters, we use the following procedure:

1. Obtain a large piece of oak tag (about 8″ by 11″).

2. Print one large letter using strokes about 1″ thick on each sheet. (The letters can also be written on sandpaper for finger tracing.)

3. Present the letter <u>c</u> and say, "This is the symbol that makes the sound (k)." (Follow with instructions on page 26 for introduction of the letter.) "I am going to write that letter on your paper and then you will:

   a) Trace what I did."

   b) Copy it all by yourself and be sure to fill the whole <u>little red house</u> (page 11)."

   c) "The letter you just wrote is called <u>c</u>."

In like manner, introduce each letter.

This chapter covers simple, phonetic consonant-short vowel-consonant words. We follow with compound words using the above and consonant-vowel-consonant detached syllables as an introduction to reading multisyllabic words.

C (hard — as in c<u>a</u>t)

Visual — Auditory

The letter is <u>c</u> as in c<u>at</u>. When dictating this letter, a key word must be given to differentiate it from the letter <u>k</u>. When the phonetic card is shown to the child, he responds with the sound of hard <u>c</u> (k). An additional help is to have the child place his head and arm on a large sheet of paper on the desk. With magic marker trace around child's arm as he holds it in a <u>c</u> position. Tack in front of room.

Kinesthetic

Put a rubber band on the wrist of the child's left hand. Have the child put his left arm on his head and touch his right ear with his hand. Then, he writes the letter. When the teacher stands in front of the room, she demonstrates the <u>mirror-image</u> of the position. The letter starts from the ear, follows the left arm and goes under the chin. It fills the whole little red house, but it does not complete the circle.

 O (as in <u>o</u>live)

Visual — Auditory

As an introduction, ask the students, "Have you ever had a sore throat? When the doctor looks into your mouth and tells you to open wide and say (ŏ), you make the correct sound and your mouth makes the shape of the letter." Should the sound be unclear, you say "I cannot see your tonsils yet." This should help the child to produce the sound properly. The teacher points a finger to her open mouth as a clue when the child forgets the sound. A tongue depresser with an *o* written on it can be an additional clue.

Kinesthetic

Manuscript

O starts at the right ear, turns to the drum and fills the whole little red house with the circle.

Cursive

We explain to the children that the difference between cursive and manuscript is that, in the cursive, the letters reach for each other and touch. We use the game "London Bridge" to illustrate this. Have two children, each representing a letter, stand in front of the room and reach out, holding both hands to build a bridge.

In most letters, "London Bridge is <u>falling down</u>." We say that in the letters <u>o</u>, <u>b</u>, <u>v</u>, and <u>w</u> the bridge is all built up.

 a (as in apple)

Visual – Auditory

The following introduction is suggested for this sound: "Tomorrow we are going to learn something new. For that you are to remember to bring an apple." The next day, tell the children that you are going to have a contest. Have them take a big bite out of the apple—the person who bites off the biggest piece is the winner. Next, each one is to open his mouth as wide as he can and make the sound (ă). From then on, for the child who forgets, you say, "A nice, big, red, juicy, delicious ă-ă-apple!"

Kinesthetic

Have the child put his left arm on his head and touch his right ear with his hand. (The teacher demonstrates.) The letter a starts from the ear, follows the left arm towards the "drum and stick" to make a circle and fills the whole little red house. Without lifting the pencil, the line with a tail is added to the circle.

 d

Many students experience confusion with the letter d. The proper kinesthetic formation of the letter plus the accompanying verbalization help to alleviate the problem.

Visual — Auditory

When the phonetic card is shown for the letter d, be sure to introduce this sound as a final consonant, as in had, to avoid the common error of saying (dǔ).

Kinesthetic

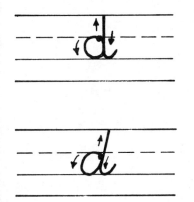

Suggested introduction to the sound: "You know what a drumstick is like, so be sure to make the drum first and then the stick. Starting at the right ear and turning to the 'drum and stick', you form the circle first. Then you go straight up to the attic and down the attic stairs again" and add the tail.

 g (hard – as in <u>go</u>)

Visual – Auditory

Advertisers use simple melodies to associate with their products. "G-go" is repeated several times in a simple tune. A common error is to call it (j). Should the child make this mistake, explain that it makes that sound sometimes, but we are not using it now.

Kinesthetic

<u>G</u> starts like <u>a</u>, at the right ear, turns to the drum—and around it goes—filling the whole red house, then down to the cellar and turns to the drum again.

m

Visual — Auditory

As the card is presented, the teacher produces the sound. The child imitates it and is told to notice how his lips tickle when he makes it.

Kinesthetic

M fills the whole little red house and makes three strokes. Count 1 - 2 - 3 and have the child tap out the rhythm on his arm with his hand. This is done because children frequently confuse m with n.

Visual – Auditory

Present the phonetic card. The teacher makes the sound. Have the student prolong the sound of the letter to protect him from saying (ĕl).

Kinesthetic

Manuscript

Start in the attic and go down to the floor of the little red house.

Cursive

Make a loop that goes up to the attic and crosses at the ceiling of the little red house.

Visual — Auditory

The sound is taught by initiating a discussion with the children. Ask if anyone has a puppy dog or has a friend who has one. Have them talk about it briefly. Then say, "I am sure you have seen such a puppy run and play so much that, when he was tired, he flopped down on his fat tummy, stuck out his little pink tongue and panted, h-h-h." Henceforth, this is called the "puppy dog sound." As a clue, the teacher pants or says, "puppy dog."

Kinesthetic

Manuscript

H starts in the attic and turns to the bat and ball as it fills the whole red house.

Cursive

Start with the l loop and fill the little red house with the hump.

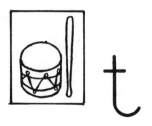 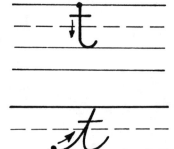 

Visual — Auditory

Be sure to use t̲ as a final consonant in your introduction—as in bat. Be sure it is not pronounced (tŭ). Should the pupil say (tŭ), correct him by telling him "to make it pure."

Kinesthetic

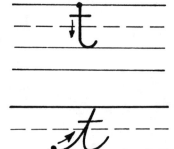

T̲ starts in the attic, goes into the little red house, turns to the bat and is crossed in the attic.

The following words use only the first nine sounds taught. We consistently apply the procedure of:

1. The teacher says the word.
2. The child repeats the word.
3. The child spells out loud.
4. The child names each letter or sounds it as he writes it.
5. After a group of words has been spelled and written, the child reads them from flash cards.

Phonetic Words for Spelling and Reading

dad	had	am	cat
Tam	Tad	hag	tag
at	cam*	ham	dam
mad	mat	hat	cad
hog	got	Tod	dot
Dom	hot	hod	cot
cod	cog	mom	Tom
Mag	lad	log	lot
lam*		tot	

The pronunciations used in this book are standard English. Some pupils and teachers may use different pronunciations for words such as log and dog. If this presents a problem for the pupil, the teacher should omit these words in the beginning stages until he thinks that the child can cope with the regional variations. We find that this is seldom a problem in teaching because pupil and teacher seem naturally to modify the enunciation to sound like their own speech.

*cam — projection on a piece of machinery adapted to impart motion to another piece
*lam — to flee; to escape

Phonetic Phrases for Dictation and Reading

a hot ham   got a cat
mad at dad   had a mat

Phonetic Sentences for Dictation and Reading

The phonetic words in these sentences use only the first nine sounds. Nonphonetic words are underlined. These should be written separately on cards and presented for the student to copy when he writes and spells from dictation. Underline them on the sentence cards also, and identify them for the child as he reads each sentence.

All sight words—including phonetic words whose sounds come later in the sequence—are underlined in the phrases and sentences through page 61. Thereafter, underlining continues until a word has appeared in five different lessons, or until all its sounds have been learned. Sight word drill is deferred until later in the program (see page 72).

1. Dictate the sentence.
2. The child repeats it.
3. The child writes the sentence.
4. The child reads the sentences from printed cards.

Tom got hot.
The log got hot.
Dot had a hot mat.
Dad is mad at Tad.
The hog got the ham.
Dad got mad at the lad.
Mom got mad at the cat.

Phonetic Reader
Alphabet Series I, #1.

36

INTRODUCING NEW SOUNDS

After the first group of nine letters has been introduced, subsequent ones are presented one at a time. Each new sound is followed by words and sentences that encompass all the sounds learned up to that point.

Each letter is thoroughly learned and competency in its application is acquired before a new letter or sound is added to the group. It is important to adhere closely to the sequence as it is given, as each step in the development depends upon the preceding one.

Enough varied drill, preferably in the form of games, should be used to insure smooth and self-assured application of the principles learned.

 (as in <u>I</u>ndian)

Visual — Auditory

This is frequently found to be a difficult sound to learn. The index finger pointing upward is used as the signal and attention is drawn to the similarity of its shape to the letter. You then suggest that the sound "seems to go to the top of the head and you can even feel it coming out."

Kinesthetic

<u>I</u> starts from the top, fills the little red house and puts a dot in the attic.

Phonetic Words for Spelling and Reading

hit	lid	it	Tim
dig	dim	mid	hid
him	did	lit	

Phonetic Phrases for Dictation and Reading

hid <u>a</u> lid

hit <u>a</u> lad

lit <u>a</u> log

Tim did it

Phonetic Sentences for Dictation and Reading

Dot hid <u>the</u> lid.

Mag lit <u>the</u> log.

Did <u>the</u> lad hit him?

Did Dom dig <u>a</u> dam?

Dad got <u>a</u> cat <u>for</u> Tim.

Phonetic Reader

Alphabet Series I,# 2.

 j

Visual — Auditory

The day before this lesson the teacher tells the class that tomorrow they are going to learn a new letter with the help of some jam. They are asked to take a vote on the flavor that they wish to have. The next day the teacher brings the jam, spreads it on a paper plate and has each child trace the letter j with his finger in the jam. They can feel the jam on their hands and are asked to talk about it. The sound becomes j-j-juicy j-j-jam.

Kinesthetic

Manuscript

J starts in the little red house, runs down to the cellar and turns to the drum.

Cursive

J starts like an i. The loop goes to the cellar and crosses on the floor of the little red house.

Phonetic Words for Spelling and Reading

(Tell the child to note that j never ends a word.)

jam	Jim	jag	jig
jog	jot		

Phonetic Phrases for Dictation and Reading

got jam   jig and jog
hid Jim

Phonetic Sentences for Dictation and Reading

Jim hid the jam.
Did Tim jig and jog?
Mom had a lot of jam.

Phonetic Reader

Alphabet Series I, # 3.

k

Visual – Auditory

In teaching this sound, be careful not to say (kŭ).

Kinesthetic

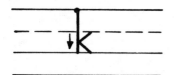

Manuscript

<u>K</u> starts in the attic. Put a dot in the middle of the red house and extend from it to the top and bottom of the red house.

Cursive

<u>H</u> goes straight down, but <u>k</u> comes back to kiss the dot.

Phonetic Words for Spelling and Reading

kid   kit   Kim

Phonetic Phrases for Dictation and Reading

hit <u>a</u> kid
hid <u>K</u>im

Phonetic Sentences for Dictation and Reading

Did Kim hit <u>the</u> kid?
<u>A</u> kit did jig.

We now have two symbols for the (k) sound. To avoid confusion, or the necessity to guess, show the appropriate card or simply state whether a <u>c</u> or a <u>k</u> is used in the spelling of the particular word. This should be done until hard and soft <u>c</u> are taught.

Phonetic Reader
Alphabet Series I, # 4.

 p

Visual — Auditory

Be sure to use p as a final consonant to avoid the common error of pronouncing it as (pŭ). Help him to visualize a dripping faucet that says, "drip-drip-drip." Also, hold a piece of tissue in front of the mouth: if the sound is made correctly, it will make the paper move.

Kinesthetic

P starts in the little red house, runs down the basement stairs, runs up the same stairs again and turns to the bat. It is found that letters that go down are more difficult to do than those that stay between two parallel lines and those that go up.

Phonetic Words for Spelling and Reading

pig	gap	pad	Pam
hip	cap	pat	lop*
pod	tap	Jip	Hap
Kip	pot	hop	mop
top	cop	lip	lap
pom-pom			

Phonetic Phrases for Dictation and Reading

pat a pig
a hot pot

pat Pam
tap Hap

Phonetic Sentences for Dictation and Reading

The cop got hot.
Did Kip tap Jip?
Did Hap pat the pig?
The top of the pot is hot.
The cap had a pom-pom.

*lop — to cut off; to trim

Phonetic Reader

Alphabet Series I, # 5.

41

 ch (as in <u>ch</u>in)

A digraph is a group of two successive letters whose phonetic value is a single sound. It is introduced to the child by saying: "W h e n t h e s e t w o l e t t e r s a r e p a r t n e r s, t h e y m a k e a s i n g l e n e w s o u n d. W h e n t w o l e t t e r s a r e p a r t n e r s a n d m a k e a s p e c i a l s o u n d, t h e y a r e c a l l e d <u>d i g r a p h</u> s." If the child has difficulty in grasping the concept of digraphs, underline the digraphs on the word cards with a black marker.

Visual — Auditory

The teacher says, "Choo-choo train" while she moves both arms like a locomotive.

Phonetic Words for Spelling and Reading

<u>Ch</u>ad	<u>ch</u>at	<u>ch</u>ip	<u>ch</u>it*
<u>ch</u>op	<u>ch</u>ap	<u>ch</u>it-<u>ch</u>at	

Phonetic Phrases for Dictation and Reading

had <u>a</u> chat   had <u>a</u> cap
chop <u>a</u> log

Phonetic Sentences for Dictation and Reading

<u>The</u> chap had <u>a</u> cap.
Did <u>the</u> chap chop <u>a</u> log?
Chad <u>and</u> Tom had <u>a</u> chat.
Did Kip <u>and</u> Dot chit-chat?

*chit—a note or bill telling what is owed, as to sign a chit for a meal instead of paying cash

Phonetic Reader
Alphabet Series I, # 6.

 (as in u̲p̲)

Visual – Auditory

The teacher clasps her hands at the level of her abdomen to form the shape of the letter u̲. As she hits her stomach with her clasped hands, she makes the sound (ŭ). The students imitate her.

Kinesthetic

Phonetic Words for Spelling and Reading

gum	gut	chug	dug
hug	mug	tug	jug
pug	dud	cud	mud
hum	hut	up	chum
cut	lug	jut	

Phonetic Phrases for Dictation and Reading

chip a̲ mug   cut a̲ mat
lug a̲ log   dug it up

Phonetic Sentences for Dictation and Reading

Jip dug up a̲ mug.
Hap dug a̲ mud hut.
Did Kip cut the̲ ham?
Did the̲ lad lug the̲ log?
The̲ top of̲ the̲ jug is̲ cut.
Chad got a̲ mug and̲ a̲ cup.

Phonetic Reader
Alphabet Series I, # 7.

 b

Visual — Auditory

When teaching this sound, be very careful to introduce it as a final consonant in order to prevent the child from saying (bŭ). Since body motions are frequently used to associate the symbol with the sounds, the teacher points her finger at the child, using it as a toy gun, and says, "The robber tries to rob-b-b." Pointing the finger becomes the hand-signal clue.

Kinesthetic

Manuscript

<u>B</u> starts in the attic, goes into the red house, and the big, round, fat tummy goes to the b-bat and the b-ball.

Cursive

The loop swings to the attic and crosses exactly on the ceiling of the red house and continues to fill the red house.

Phonetic Words for Spelling and Reading

bag	bad	bit	job
cob	bog	bat	bud
bid	jab	big	but
tab	dub	tub	hub
bug	pub	Lib	dab
Bim	Bob	lob	

Phonetic Phrases for Dictation and Reading

<u>a</u> big bag   jab Bob
bit <u>a</u> bug   <u>a</u> bad job

Phonetic Sentences for Dictation and Reading

Lib got a job.
Bob lit the log.
The bag is big.
Bim got the cab.
Pam got a big tip.
Tom got a big top.
Bob and Kim chat a lot.

Phonetic Reader
Alphabet Series I, # 8

The (r) sound is practiced in the initial position to prevent it from being pronounced as (ĕr).

Kinesthetic

Cursive

R starts like an i and should stay in the little red house, but by accident gets over the line just a teeny bit and—oops—it goes right back to the line, travels a little bit along the ceiling and down it goes where it belongs, into the little red house.

Phonetic Words for Spelling and Reading

ram	rim	rap	rat
rip	rib	rig	rob
rot	rag	rut	rich
rub	rod	rug	

Phonetic Phrases for Dictation and Reading

a rich lad   a rag rug
rip a rag   rub a log

Phonetic Sentences for Dictation and Reading

Pat the ram.
The rat bit the hog.
Did Rob rub the rod?
Did the ram rip the rag?
The rim of the pot is big.
The rich chap got a big rug.

Phonetic Readers
Alphabet Series I, # 9 and # 10.

 f

Visual – Auditory – Tactile

Teach the child to put his hand in front of his face and to blow on it so that he can <u>feel</u> the sound on his hand. The hand in front of the teacher's face becomes a clue.

Kinesthetic

Manuscript

<u>F</u> starts in the attic and goes into the little red house.

Cursive

The loop swings to the attic and crosses exactly on the ceiling of the red house. It continues down to the basement. The bottom loop goes up on the same side as the one above and stops at the floor of the little red house.

Phonetic Words for Spelling and Reading

fib	fad	fit	fob*
fat	fig	fog	

Phonetic Phrases for Dictation and Reading

<u>a</u> fat pig   <u>a</u> big fig
<u>a</u> bad fit

Phonetic Sentences for Dictation and Reading

Pat <u>the</u> fat pig.
<u>The</u> hat fit Dot.
<u>Is</u> it bad <u>to</u> fib?
Jim bit <u>the</u> big fig.

*fob – a watch chain or ribbon, especially one hanging from a small pocket

 n

Visual — Auditory

If the student has trouble with the sound, tell him to wrinkle his nose as he says it.

Kinesthetic

N fills the little red house and goes 1—2 strokes downward.

Phonetic Words for Spelling and Reading

Lon	nag	Dan	gun
Don	fan	fun	man
not	Jan	bun	nod
can	ran	nip	chin
fin	din	tin	bin
pan	pin	pun	nut
		on	nab

Phonetic Phrases for Dictation and Reading

not a pin

a man ran

a tin pan

nip a chin

Phonetic Sentences for Dictation and Reading

Tom can jig.
Pat can nag.
Dan is not bad.
Fan the hot pan.
Pin the tag on Jan.
Jim ran to the man.
The pup can nip Don.
The bun is on a hot pan.
The cop can nab the man.

Phonetic Reader
Alphabet Series I, #11.

 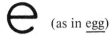 e (as in egg)

Visual – Auditory

This sound frequently presents difficulty. If the students are young and the letter is being introduced for the first time, read Dr. Seuss's book <u>Horton Hatches the Egg</u> substituting "Ed" for the elephant's name. Tell the children this is a story for learning the sound (ĕ). Everytime you say "egg," "Ed," or "elephant," you tell the children to say (ĕ) in unison.

If the book is unavailable, have a relay race with a hard-boiled egg or the children can sing a chant, "There once was an ĕ-ĕ-ĕ-elephant whose name was ĕ-ĕ-ĕ-Ed and he sat on an ĕ-ĕ-ĕ-egg."

Kinesthetic

Cursive

The loop fills the whole little red house.

Phonetic Words for Spelling and Reading

get	men	Ben	keg
den	bet	bed	beg
peg	hep	leg	Deb
fed	hen	let	hem
met	ten	net	pet
pen	Meg	Peg	

Phonetic Phrases for Dictation and Reading

in a pen

on a hen

met ten men

pet can beg

Phonetic Sentences for Dictation and Reading

Ben met ten men.

Jip did not get fed.

Meg let the pet beg.

Peg got a rip on the hem.

The pet hen is in the pen.

Phonetic Reader

Alphabet Series I, # 12 and # 13.

S (as in s̲i̲t)

Visual – Auditory

S̲ is shaped like a snake and hisses like a snake.

Kinesthetic

'S

Manuscript

This is an easily reversed letter. It starts from the bat, curves halfway down the red house and then cùrves in the opposite direction.

Cursive

S̲ starts like an i̲, comes to a point like an arrow and curves right back to where it started.

Phonetic Words for Spelling and Reading

sag	sad	Sam	sat
sit	such	sap	sip
sop	sup	sub	sum
sin	sun	Sid	Sol
Sal	sot*	sib*	

Phonetic Sentences for Dictation and Reading

Sam got ten men.
Sal sat in the̲ sun.
Sid i̲s̲ such a̲ sad man.
The̲ men can sit in the̲ sun.
I̲ can sit in the̲ sun and̲ sip.

*sot – a drunkard
*sib – a blood relation

Phonetic Readers
Alphabet Series I, # 15 and # 16.

 sh

This is a digraph—two letters together which make a special sound. If the child has difficulty in grasping the concept of digraphs, underline them in black on the word cards.

Visual — Auditory

Make the sound and put a finger on the lips to indicate quiet.

Phonetic Words for Spelling and Reading

shad	shun	sham	shop
shot	shag	mash	shed
shim*	shin	dish	dash
ship	shod	shut	sash
cash	bash	hash	rash
lash	gash	gosh	fish
josh	mesh	mush	

Phonetic Sentences for Dictation and Reading

I can mash shad.
Sal had a red sash.
The men shut the shop.
Peg hit Bob on the shin.
The cash is in the shop.
Ned got a dish for the dog.
The gash on the ship is big.
I can mash the ham in the pot.

*shim—a thin wedge of wood used to fill a space or make something level, as in leveling up a building stone or making a railroad tie level

 **th** (hard — as in <u>th</u>at)

Another digraph sound—two letters together which make a special sound. If the child has difficulty in grasping the concept of digraphs, underline them in black on the word cards.

Visual — Auditory

Stick your tongue between the biting edges of your teeth to make this sound.

Phonetic Words for Spelling and Reading

that	than	them
then	thus	this

Phonetic Sentences for Dictation and Reading

Hit that cat.
Pat that man.
This ship <u>is</u> hit.
Sam got them <u>to</u> shut <u>the</u> shop.
<u>The</u> men can sit on this big mat.

Phonetic Reader
Alphabet Series I, # 16.

 W

Visual — Auditory

"How can you tell when a dog is friendly and happy?" "W-wag" and move the hand as though a dog is wagging its tail.

Kinesthetic

Phonetic Words for Spelling and Reading

win	wit	wet	web
wed	wag	wig	wen*
with	wish		

Phonetic Sentences for Dictation and Reading

It is fun to win.
The wet wig fit Meg.
A web on a bed is bad.
It is fun to run with them.
A dog can wag and be mad.
Ted and Jim wish to win the bet.

*wen — a tumor of the skin

 wh

Visual – Auditory

Pronounced backwards, it makes the sound (h-w). Since most people do not pronounce it correctly, they do not spell it correctly. If you remember that it is pronounced (h-w), you will never forget the <u>h</u>. Tell the children to feel their breath blowing on their hands as they say <u>whistle</u>. If a child has difficulty in grasping the concept of digraphs, underline them in black on the word cards.

Phonetic Words for Spelling and Reading

whim	which	when	whet
whit	whip	whin*	whish*
whop			

Phonetic Sentences for Dictation and Reading

It <u>is</u> bad <u>to</u> whip <u>a</u> lad.
When can <u>the</u> dog get fed?
Which rod <u>is</u> on <u>the</u> rug?
Sam did not wish <u>to</u> whip him.
Which wig did Pam wish <u>to</u> get?

*whish – to move with a swishing sound
*whin – any particularly hard rock

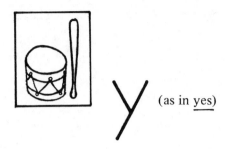

y (as in yes)

Visual — Auditory

We ask the children, "Would you like a million dollars?" The answer is, "Y as in yes."

Kinesthetic

Cursive

Y starts like a u and goes down to the basement to make a loop.

Phonetic Words for Spelling and Reading

yes	yap	yip	yak*
yon	yam	yet	yen

Phonetic Sentences for Dictation and Reading

Did Jim get wet yet?
The yam is in the pan.
Did the yak yap at the cat?
Tom had a yen to run.

Phonetic Reader
Alphabet Series I, # 17.

*yak — a giant ox found in Asia

56

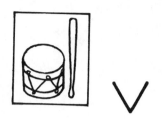 V

Visual – Auditory

Have the child shape two fingers like a v̲ or put his elbow on the table.

Kinesthetic

Cursive

V̲ reaches for the next letter as in "London Bridge is all built up."

Phonetic Words for Spelling and Reading

van   vat   vim   Val
vet

Phonetic Sentences for Dictation and Reading

Get in the̲ van.
Which cat sat on the̲ van?
Val did not wish to̲ get the̲ vat wet.

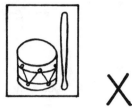
X

Visual — Auditory

Be sure it is pronounced (ks). When the teacher dictates the sound for drill, she says, "(ks) as in box."

Kinesthetic

X   𝒳

Phonetic Words for Spelling and Reading

ax	box	fix	mix
fox	lox*	lax	six
wax	tax	ox	Max
vex			

Phonetic Sentences for Dictation and Reading

Fix the box.
Jan had a bit of lox.
Max had wax on his ax.
The ox and the fox sat on a box.
Tom is lax and did not wax the ax.

*lox—smoked salmon

Z

Visual — Auditory

"You go z-z-zig, and you go z-z-zag."

Kinesthetic

Manuscript

<u>Z</u> starts from the drum and stick and goes to the bat and ball — like the number <u>7</u>. If the children have not learned the number <u>7</u>, this will facilitate the learning of both symbols.

Cursive

Start by making the top part of the number <u>3</u> in the little red house. Go down to the basement and make a loop.

Phonetic Words for Spelling and Reading

whiz	zip	zax*	zig-zag
zed*	zep	zel*	

Phonetic Sentences for Dictation and Reading

Zip it on.
Val <u>is a</u> whiz with an ax.
Val <u>can</u> zig-zag with vim.
It <u>is</u> fun <u>to go</u> up in <u>a</u> zep.
<u>The</u> bug had <u>a</u> yen <u>to</u> zig-zag.
Tom can fix <u>the</u> top <u>of the</u> shed with <u>a</u> zax.

*zax — a tool for roofing
*zed — a name for the letter <u>z</u>, chiefly British usage
*zel — a kind of cymbal

59

 **th** (soft – <u>second</u> <u>choice</u> – as in <u>thin</u>)

This is another digraph—two letters together which make a special sound. If the child has difficulty in grasping the concept of digraphs, underline them in black on the word cards.

Visual – Auditory

To help the child who has difficulty making the sound, instruct him to let the tip of the tongue come out between the teeth.

Phonetic Words for Spelling and Reading

thin   bath   thug
thud   path

Phonetic Sentences for Dictation and Reading

<u>The</u> thin cat had <u>a</u> bath.
<u>The</u> ax hit <u>the</u> box with <u>a</u> thud.
<u>The</u> thug ran with <u>a</u> bag <u>of</u> cash.
<u>The</u> dog led <u>the</u> man up <u>the</u> path.

qu  (as in queen)

Q never goes anywhere without u.

Kinesthetic

Phonetic Words for Spelling and Reading

quit	quiz	quip
quid*	quag*	

Phonetic Sentences for Dictation and Reading

Sam got the vet to quit.
Max had a whiz of a quiz.
It is fun to quip with that man.

Phonetic Reader
Alphabet Series I, # 20.

*quag — soft marshy land
*quid — a portion suitable to be chewed — a quid of tobacco

After all the letters have been introduced, we want to be sure that the student is proficient and secure in the use of three-letter phonetic words before we continue. Review lists are used to test his skills. Should he have trouble making a perfect score on the first review list, more time should be spent on the material as follows:

1. Review phonetic word cards.
2. Dictate sentences which the child then reads from a printed card.
3. Have him read different books that are written on the same level.
4. Play word games.
5. Recheck with another review list.

TACHISTOSCOPE

Some children have trouble separating figure from ground and, therefore, have difficulty reading words from a list. The review list should be given to them through the use of a tachistoscope so that they can see one word at a time.

Instructions for Making a Tachistoscope

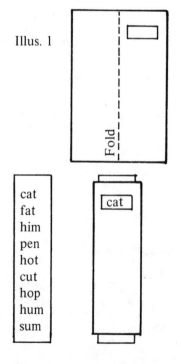

Illus. 1

Illus. 2   Illus. 3

Use a standard manila folder:

1. Measure 2-1/2 inches from the folded edge and cut a strip the length of the folder.
2. Open flat and cut a window 2 inches from the top on the right half of the strip. It should be large enough to expose one word at a time. See illustration 1.
3. Tape the open sides together.
4. Cut 1 inch off the bottom of the tachistoscope. The tachistoscope should be at least 1 inch shorter than the strip. See illustration 2.
5. Use the rest of the manila folder to cut strips that will pull through the tachistoscope.
6. Use a primer typewriter to type review lists on these strips. Be sure that the words are double- or triple-spaced so that only one word at a time is exposed through the window. See illustration 3.

REVIEW TESTS

CONSONANT-VOWEL-CONSONANT WORDS

The student should be proficient in review tests before continuing to the next step in the sequence. If he is able to read and spell the words in column a easily, continue with the next step in the sequence. If not, take time out to review the preceding materials, and then try column b, etc.

a	b	c	d
hath	Vic	rob	wet
sop	chop	Kim	rub
ax	map	hap	nip
cog	rug	rich	quag
cut	bin	quid	yet
dim	let	fez	cud
rod	yes	sun	when
fix	whig	jug	zip
shun	tax	wish	shod
lav	rob	ox	Val
lash	zag	thug	such
which	hut	six	wax
win	hug	whit	him
rub	jot	yet	sob
wet	shed	van	kid
mop	box	don	ram
fen	wax	men	then
bun	fish	cob	hog
yak	kith	but	tub
fed	quip	lap	fan
quiz	them	hush	job
sit	lush	fed	vim

TWO-SYLLABLE COMPOUND WORDS

Show the child that big words <u>can be</u> easy to read. Have the child read the first syllable, then the second, and finally the word. If child is ready, the syllable technique on pages 70 and 109 may be introduced at this time.

Word cards for compounds should show the compound word divided on one side and written as one word on the other. For example:

pig pen	pigpen

Pupils should be shown the divided word first and then the other side of the card with the word written normally. Compounds on the sentence cards should not be shown divided.

Phonetic Words for Spelling and Reading

can not	sun set	sun fish
up set	cat nip	with in
gun men	sun tan	mix up
pig pen	dish pan	in let
gun man	bed bug	whip lash
up shot	bob cat	mid ship
hot rod	Bat man	ram rod
pen man	cat fish	ash can

Phonetic Sentences for Dictation and Reading

The den is dim at sunset.
The shot upset the gunmen.
Jim cannot sit in the pigpen.
<u>He</u> got Max a box of catnip.

SPELLING RULE – ff-ll-ss

Words of one syllable ending in <u>f</u>, <u>l</u>, or <u>s</u>, usually end in double <u>ff</u>, <u>ll</u>, or <u>ss</u>; that is, make <u>f</u>, <u>l</u>, and <u>s</u> "twins" at the end of a short word.

This simple rule increases the reading and spelling vocabulary without the necessity of learning new sounds. While this rule is being practiced, keep the illustrated chart in front of the students.

ff - ll - ss

Dictate for spelling first and then have the student read the following from cards.

doll	fell	gull	mass
null	hill	yell	puff
biff	less	hull	lass
miff	muss	dill	buff
bill	bass	will	kill
muff	moss	sell	mess
dell	pill	huff	till
well	lull	kiss	fill
hell	mill	sill	ill
bell	fuss	tell	cull
doff	fill	cuff	hiss
mull	dull	whiff	quill
chaff*	quell	chess	

Phonetic Sentences for Dictation and Reading

The man fell in the dell.
Less moss is less mess.
Ben will fuss if <u>you</u> kiss him.
Can Bill fill the cup with dill?
Tell Biff to get a bill <u>for</u> the pill.
Let Ted tell the men to get a bell.
Can <u>you</u> sell the chess set to Will?

*chaff – to make fun of in a good-natured way; the husks of grain separated from the seed by threshing

65

A single s̲ at the end of several short words is pronounced (z) for reading, as are the plurals of many words.

Examples for Dictation and Spelling

is	his	lids
as	has	rags

I am as big as his dad is.
Has the cat got his hat?

DETACHED SYLLABLES

After the child has mastered the skill of applying newly learned sounds for reading three- or four-letter words, we begin the study of three- or four-letter phonetic syllables.

Our detached syllables are always parts of real words, never "nonsense" syllables. They perform two important functions:

1. They provide an excellent test to demonstrate whether the child can read the phonic symbols when they appear in unfamiliar combinations.
2. The child is prepared for future reading of polysyllabic words.

Put a list of syllables on the blackboard, and beside it, a list of words in which they occur. Examples can be selected from the list printed below. It is important to use words that are appropriate for the age of the child.

Explain that syllables are parts of words. Help the student notice that each syllable must have a vowel by asking "What is it that all these syllables have in common?" Deal only with the <u>first</u> syllables in polysyllabic words for this actviity.

Detached Syllables	Suggested Words (For Teacher's Use)
dom	dominate
dem	democrat
tel	telephone
hap	happen
mem.	member
dif	different
dic	dictate
suf	suffer
	(continued)

Detached Syllables		Suggested Words (For Teacher's Use)
jus	im	justice
tum	in	tumble
choc	ex	chocolate
riv	ad	river
tad	ab	tadpole
dis	es	disturb
doc	un	doctor
fab	um	fabulous
sil	ob	silver
tal	on	talcum
sev		several
lib		liberal
whis		whisper
sub		submarine
med		medicine
hab		habit
mis		mistake
tem		temple

Put the following list of syllables on the blackboard and have the children give examples of words in which they appear, if they can think of any. These syllables should be given for spelling and then read individually from cards.

bam	gog	nal	lat
tal	fas	heb	vol
jan	hap	pab	sud
viv	suf	pov	sab
nam	siz	rus	lan
ben	col	cus	whis
dex	nex	vix	ped
com	bon	tac	chas

Many children enjoy having detached syllables dictated in sentence form, a few detached syllables at a time. Designate the end of a sentence by a rising or a lowering inflection, or in an exclamatory tone. The child then ends the sentence with a period, question mark, or an exclamation point.

Learning these three simple punctuation marks is an easily acquired skill that can assist in reading with expression. It is sometimes helpful to use different colors for each punctuation mark.

REVIEW TESTS

CONSONANT-VOWEL-CONSONANT DETACHED SYLLABLES

The student should be proficient in review tests before continuing to the next step in the sequence. If he is able to read and spell the words in column a easily, continue with the next step in the sequence. If not, take time out to review the preceding materials, and then try column b, etc.

a	b	c	d
wog	guz	quib	wiz
pon	whis	yuc	duc
dom	thim	gog	hab
zith	ques	lan	ren
fes	rus	whil	tel
kaf	hap	mam	sem
tac	ex	chas	shuf
bon	com	dif	mis
sub	dic	fal	vid
quil	vom	jus	med
rud	tep	pov	kin
tem	lob	kil	vol
choc	riv	ses	tad
nex	wid	con	dis
nov	cal	doc	yon
viv	fab	zep	pol
hib	yon	hom	sug
jag	kan	bux	raf
yel	jun	shiv	chat
hud	dex	ret	jux

CHAPTER VI

INTRODUCING TWO-SYLLABLE WORDS

TWO-SYLLABLE WORDS

After teaching detached syllables, present them in two-syllable words. The children derive special pleasure from the ability to read successfully unusual and unfamiliar words.

The transition to words of more than one syllable is a big step to the young student or the student who has experienced reading difficulty. He should be shown how easily the detached syllables can be formed into "big words."

The following exercise is a helpful device:

1. Print the two syllables of a word on two separate index cards. Have the child read the first card, the second card, and then the two in sequence, blending them into a word.

   Example: bon   net
                     tan   dem
                     vel   vet
                     tin   sel

2. Place the two syllables of a word in a large envelope. Have the student empty the envelope, read both detached syllables and juggle them to make a word.
3. After he has done the above with ease, empty two, three, or four syllable cards at once and ask him to make as many two-syllable words as he can from the jumbled parts.

Two-Syllable Phonetic Words for Spelling and Reading

These should be read first from cards and then from a list.

The student may use purely phonetic or exaggerated pronunciation for the unstressed final syllables in such words as <u>linden</u>, <u>velvet</u> and <u>tonsil</u>, and then modify them when necessary to arrive at a "normal" way of speaking.

In first dictating such a word, the teacher could pronounce it two ways: "normal" and then exaggerated to make the vowel clearer, for example, "linden— lĭn dĕn."

lin den	pos sum	pep lum*	bod kin*
wom bat*	nap kin	bas ket	cac tus
nut meg	can did	tab let	tal cum
vel vet	pep sin	gob lin	ton sil
pic nic	ban dit	pub lic	tid bit
hum bug	ham let	sub mit	ram rod
tan dem	pop lin	ban yan*	lit mus*
sam pan*	hob nob	hic cup	wit less
vic tim	van quish	wit ness	

Phonetic Sentences for Reading

The bit of nutmeg is in a napkin.
Jill and Meg will picnic at sunset.
She had a velvet sash on the basket.
The men in the hamlet got the bandit a gun.
The catnip on the cactus is a tidbit <u>for</u> the cat.

*peplum — a short skirt attached to a blouse or coat
*bodkin — a sharp implement for making holes, especially in cloth
*wombat — a burrowing animal of Australia
*banyan — a large East Indian tree from whose branches many roots grow downward and form new trunks
*sampan — a small boat used in the harbors of China and Japan
*litmus — a dyestuff obtained from certain lichens which turns red in an acid and blue in a base.

SIGHT VOCABULARY

In the sentences that are given for dictation and reading, there are underlined words which may be considered sight words. When the child is reading, the teacher identifies the underlined word for him. When the teacher dictates sentences, a card containing the underlined word is placed in front of him. In this way he will automatically learn some of these words.

At this point in the sequence the following sight words have appeared five or more times:

a	is	the
and	of	to
for		

Others commonly used later in the book include:

be	go	was	you
do	have	what	your
from	he	are	
we	off	were	

After he has acquired basic phonic skills, greater emphasis can be placed on developing his sight vocabulary. For this purpose, we recommend using the Dolch Sight Cards which consist of:

> Popper Words — Sets 1 and 2
> Basic Sight Vocabulary Cards
> Sight Phrase Cards

These can be ordered from:

> Garrard Publishing Co.
> 1607 N. Market Street
> Champaign, Illinois 61820

INTRODUCING CONSONANT BLENDS

Unlike the digraph, where the two letters make one sound, each sound of a blend is heard, but the sounds are blended together.

Present consonant blends in two groups:

1. Initial Consonant Blends
2. Final Consonant Blends

Teach the student to pronounce consonant blends from flash cards and then dictate the same. The consonant blend cards will have the sound on the front and a representative word on the other side for the student to read.

1. Initial Consonant Blends

bl (blot)	fl (flag)	fr (from)	spl (split)
dr (drag)	sp (spot)	tr (trap)	scr (scrap)
sl (sled)	sw (swop)	sn (snap)	str (strip)
gr (grip)	cl (clap)	sk (skin)	shr (shrimp)
br (brass)	cr (cram)	pr (press)	sm (smash)
pl (plum)	squ (squint)	gl (glob)	st (stop)

Present groups of words in the sequence as follows:

a) Phonetic words with initial consonant blends followed by a vowel and consonant (for spelling and reading)

drip	trim	slab	drop
trip	snug	grip	skip
skin	brim	trod	frog
from	plum	grab	plot
glad	sled	snag	grim
drag	prop	drug	trap
sprig	strap	drum	step
squid	glen		

Phonetic Sentences for Dictation and Reading

Drag the sled to the shed.
Trim the skin on the drum.
Tell Glen to grip the strap.
I am glad I did not drop the frog.

b) Consonant blend – vowel – consonant digraph

plush	smash	trash	crash
flash	slush	blush	brush
flush		flesh	fresh
crush			

Phonetic Sentences for Dictation and Reading

The slush will drip <u>from</u> the step.
The cup will smash if <u>I</u> drop it.
Tell Glen to brush the big, fat cat.

c) Consonant blend followed by spelling rule <u>f f-l l-s s</u>

still	stiff	spell	swell
grass	glass	stuff	dress
press	staff	snuff	sniff
smell	brass	crass	frill
grill	scuff	scull*	trill
class	cliff	spill	floss
skiff	bless	skill	skull
shrill	thrill	scruff	stress

Phonetic Sentences for Dictation and Reading

Will Dom sniff snuff?
Can <u>you</u> press the dress?
Did Tom get a brass grill?
<u>I</u> can smell the grass.

2. Final Consonant Blends

Present these sounds on flash cards and then dictate:

nd	nt	mp	lk
lt	lp	pt	sk
st	sp	ft	nch

*scull – to propel a boat with a pair of short oars

74

Present groups of words in sequence as follows:

a) Phonetic words starting with a consonant or consonant digraph, then a vowel followed by a consonant blend

risk	chant	pulp	jump	bump
fond	shunt	quest	chest	last
vest	lent	chump	quilt	rest
list	wisp	shift	thump	fast
camp	lamp	mend	theft	bunch
milk	best	runt	hand	quint
silk	dent	dust	yelp	shelf
help	pest	bend	desk	whist
quench	tilt	land		

Phonetic Sentences for Dictation and Reading

Bill can dust the shelf.
Send the list to the class.
I am fond of the red vest.
This is the best bunch of silk.
If you bump the lamp, it will drop.
The rest of the milk is in the chest.
Can you mend the dent on the desk?

b) Words starting with a consonant blend followed by a vowel and a consonant blend

grunt	stand	crisp	bland	tramp
stamp	squint	plump	plant	crust
spent	brisk	trunk	slept	grand
clump	drift	print	splint	slant
grant	blast	brand	trust	French
stilt	branch			

Phonetic Sentences for Dictation and Reading

A crisp crust is grand.
It is fun to stand on a stilt.
The tramp slept on a soft bed.
Can you stand on the big trunk?
Stan got a splint from the branch.
Grant will plant the clump of grass.

75

REVIEW TESTS

CONSONANT BLENDS

The student should be proficient in review tests before continuing to the next step in the sequence. If he is able to read and spell the words in column a easily, continue with the next step in the sequence. If not, take time out to review the preceding materials, and then try column b, etc.

a	b	c	d
frisk	send	blush	best
wind	brag	hand	brand
grim	shrimp	milk	must
wilt	camp	gift	yelp
bump	swim	stamp	scrap
clip	press	mask	crisp
spent	blunt	grass	splint
spell	swept	flint	strand
skill	smell	shrill	skin
drug	drum	swift	trap
test	grand	vest	next
prop	drift	stilt	twist
slush	slab	drop	snuff
trip	rust	grip	still
shift	trust	brass	brim
smith	split	brisk	flash
plant	smash	trod	frog
from	plum	splash	plush
bless	lisp	lunch	grasp
scruff	strap	clasp	dress

REVIEW SENTENCES — CONSONANT BLENDS

Did Ben drop that plant?
Fred will lend Jim the sled.
The sled went off in a flash.
I still print stamps by hand.
Tell Brad to trim the grass.
I am fond of that brass band.
Tell Trish to press the dress.
We sniff snuff and smell grass.
Tell the men to mend the brass.
Do not drop the trash on the grass.
Grip the strap and do not let it drop.
Jill will be glad if you grill the lunch.
Hand Jim a slab for the top of the bench.

DETACHED SYLLABLES – CONSONANT BLENDS

Phonetic for Spelling and Reading

These detached syllables are parts of real words and are organized in the sequence of:

1. Consonant Blend – Vowel – Consonant or Consonant Digraph
2. Consonant – Vowel – Consonant Blend
3. Consonant Blend – Vowel – Consonant Blend

1. Consonant Blend – Vowel – Consonant

cred	strom	grad	grat
drom	plic	spec	gram
flim	trin	clus	stig
crat	tres	prat	plas
trop	trum	stom	swin
blan	blem	grum	blun
spon	crum	swag	stat
trag	trol	trib	cron
splin	scrib	slith	plish
drosh			

2. Consonant – Vowel – Consonant Blend

dont	dict	ject	lect
ment	sect	pend	pels
rupt	lisk	tend	vent
zond	mult	tant	ract
gant	hamp	quent	mand
nist	dapt	dopt	dult
fect	sump	tist	

3. Consonant Blend – Vowel – Consonant Blend

scond	spect	tract
trans	drant	spond
stract	brant	struct
stant	trast	prent
flict		

REVIEW TESTS

DETACHED SYLLABLES – CONSONANT BLENDS

The student should be proficient in review tests before continuing to the next step in the sequence. If he is able to read and spell the words in column a easily, continue with the next step in the sequence. If not, take time out to review the preceding materials, and then try column b, etc.

a	b	c	d
clud	clus	pend	mund
flux	ment	rupt	spect
junct	spec	tract	trans
crat	brupt	blem	grum
zond	flim	nult	grog
stant	cred	snaf	emp
spond	tral	dwin	splin
brev	splen	strep	rect
lect	mand	sput	dept
trum	flab	stron	prog
ment	blun	strat	strel
drosh	gren	tect	gram
prag	lect	dopt	drant
lusk	frip	smol	brev
tend	tres	flam	lisk
pros	mult	twen	slith
trask	dren	plish	grap
friv	swin	bris	bron
kempt	twid	trum	stin
prot	snig	swiv	hamp

TWO-SYLLABLE WORDS USING CONSONANT BLENDS

After teaching detached syllables with consonant blends, present them in two-syllable words.

1. Print each syllable of a word on a card.
   Have the child read each card.
   Have the child blend the syllables into a word.

2. Place two syllables of a word in an envelope.
   Have the child empty the envelope.
   Have him read each detached syllable.
   Have him read the word.

3. For the child who has difficulty reading these two-syllable words, even though they are divided for him, writing the syllables of the words under each other seems to help.

   Example: prob$_{lem}$ tan$_{trum}$

4. Read the following words from flash cards, tachistoscope and word lists—in that order.*

Phonetic Words for Spelling and Reading

prob lem	in spect	in vent	in sect
tan trum	in flict	ad vent	ab rupt
drag net	sus pect	tem pest	dis rupt
in ject	ob ject	en camp	sol vent
ad junct	ex pect	den tist	en gulf
sus pend	im pact	up lift	ship ment
in sult	plas tic	wind swept	with held
pump kin	traf fic	blan dish	ab stract
con test	com ment	trum pet	chump ish
un twist			

Phonetic Sentences for Reading

I like nutmeg in my milk.
A lot of traffic can be a problem.
She did not object to the plastic pumpkin.
The shipment will be withheld if you stop.
The peplum on her dress is made of tinsel.
It is not much fun to be with a chumpish man.

*See page 62 for tachistoscope instructions.

ENDINGS: <u>ing</u> – <u>ang</u> – <u>ong</u> – <u>ung</u> – <u>ink</u> – <u>ank</u> – <u>onk</u> – <u>unk</u>

These combinations of sounds are usually learned easily. They are taught as endings to simplify the breaking down of words for spelling and reading.

Present each of the following endings on a separate card with a related word on the other side.

ing – k<u>ing</u>
ang – b<u>ang</u>
ong – g<u>ong</u>
ung – h<u>ung</u>
ank – b<u>ank</u>
ink – st<u>ink</u>
onk – h<u>onk</u>
unk – s<u>unk</u>

1. Show the card – The child says "ing."
2. Turn the card over – The child reads the word – <u>king</u>.
3. Put words on the chalkboard – Cut <u>ing</u>, <u>ang</u>, etc. off with red chalk – Have the child read the word.
4. For spelling, put the <u>ing</u> card in front of the child and dictate the appropriate words and sentences.

Put the <u>ang</u> card in front of the child and dictate the words in that category. Follow the same procedure with each sound.

Practice Words

ing

king	sing	ring	wing
zing	thing	sting	swing
sling	cling	bring	string
spring			

Sentences: A frog will sing in the spring. The thing on the king is a big ring.

ang

rang	fang	gang	hang
clang	twang	sprang	bang
sang			

Sentence: Hang the bell and it will clang.

ong

In some regions there is a slight difference in the pronunciation of "ong" in these words.

ong = bong
ong = song

song	gong	long	tong
prong	strong	thong	throng
bong	wrong		

Sentence: Sing a song for King Kong.

ung

sung	hung	lung	rung
clung	stung	swung	slung
strung	sprung	dung	

Sentence: The bug stung the King.

ink

sink	kink	link	mink
pink	think	blink	stink
slink	twink	brink	drink
shrink	rink		

Sentence: I do not think I can drink ink.

ank

bank	sank	rank	tank
thank	drank	dank	Hank
lank	yank	crank	clank
plank	blank	Frank	prank
shrank			

Sentence: Hank got a blank slip from the bank.

onk

honk	conk

unk

sunk	bunk	dunk	hunk
junk	punk	funk	clunk
trunk	plunk	chunk	

Sentence: A lot of junk is in the trunk.

For review, mix words and present them for spelling and reading.

king	plank	shrink
thing	etc.	

Sentences for Dictation and Spelling

The plank sank in the tank.
Frank drank a drink with zing.
I think the king is a strong man.
You can hang the gong with string.
Tell Jill to thank the man for the ring.

Limericks and Rhymes for ing-ang-ong-ung-ink-ank-unk-onk

Children may enjoy reading the following rhymes and making up similar ones of their own. Repeated sight words will be quickly learned.

Ung

There once was a bell that hung
in the hamlet of Ung.
The birds did sing
when the bell swung and rung
in that hamlet of Ung.

Ink

There once was a cat named Ink
who had lots of milk to drink,
but then he got a kink and his tail
did shrink.

Ing

There once was a cow named Bing
who always did wish to sing.
Do you think a cow named Bing
Can sing and do her own thing?

Ang

There once was a dog named Fang
who did wish to go "bang-bang,"
but his fang got in front of his "bang."

Onk

There once was a hog named Onk
who always did wish to honk.
But when he went honk,
it came out "conk."
Oh! that sad hog named Onk.

Unk

There once was a ship named Unk
which was just a hunk of junk.
So Unk went plunk and dunk and
sunk
And that was the end of Unk.

Ank

There once was an owl named Hank
who had a dad named Frank.
Hank and dad Frank
were so wise that they went to the
bank.

Ong

There once was a town of Ong
that had a very big gong.
But do not get it wrong,
you had to be strong
to make that gong go bong.

—contributed by Janet Morabito

The concept of "magic e" is a difficult one for many children. They have learned the short form of the vowels for reading, and the name of each vowel for drill and spelling. The student has been conditioned to respond to the symbols of the vowels with a short sound. He is now asked to change his response to the established cue. When the one-syllable word ends in e, he must change his response to the long sound of the vowel.

When introducing this new sound for the vowel, we prefer to use the term "name of the vowel" rather than "long vowel," as the child has been taught that the vowel has a name and "says" a particular sound. Besides, who ever saw a long or a short letter?

Review Vowel Sounds

Before teaching "magic e," it is best to review the vowels. The following device is a helpful aid to enable the student to remember which letters are vowels.

Tell the students that tomorrow you are going to bring everyone a lollipop. The next day, put the following on blackboard or a chart.

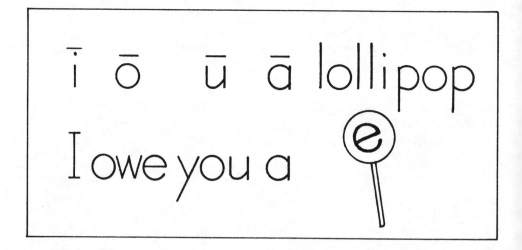

Each child is given a lollipop on which he pastes the letter e, either by writing the letter on a piece of masking tape or by cutting one out of paper and gluing it on. They are taught a trick which can make the vowel "say its name" in the words they read. The "magic e" on that lollipop is used as a magic wand. It will change a small pin into a great big pine, a kit into a kite, will make your pal pale, and, instead of a little bit of candy, you may have a great big bite.

84

1. Write on the chalkboard or on a piece of paper a three-letter word that can be changed by "magic _e_" into another word.

2. Have the child underline the vowel in red.

3. Add "magic _e_" to the end of the word and explain that this tells you to use the name of the vowel in the word.

4. Have the child read the word.

The following words can be used for this purpose.

pin	pine
kit	kite
gat	gate
tin	tine
tap	tape
not	note
mat	mate
rod	rode
rat	rate
pal	pale
rid	ride
fat	fate
nap	nape
mop	mope
bit	bite
hid	hide
Jan	Jane
mad	made
plan	plane
gap	gape

5. Make a tachistoscope for "magic e."

The three-letter words on the preceding list are typed in primer type on a strip of manila paper or written with thick magic marker on a chart for group teaching.

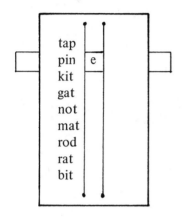

Draw two vertical lines parallel to the list and to the right of it—wide enough for the letter e to be inserted. Slit the lines dot to dot, as illustrated. Insert the strip with the letter e printed in the center in red. The child reads the word, pulls the strip to expose the letter e next to the word and, then, reads the new word.

tap
pin e
kit
gat
not
mat
rod
rat
bit

Sentences for Dictation and Reading

Jan got a bit of a bite.
You can fix the tap with tape.
Jan hid and made Jane hide.
Did Sam plan to make a plane?
The gap in the hill made them gape.
The kit will like to get the kite.

6. Write another group of four-letter words and have the child underline the vowel in red and draw an arrow from "magic e" to the vowel.

j o̲ k e

At first, this should be a two-step process.
1) Pronounce the name of vowel.
2) Read the word.

7. Do the same as above without underlining, stating that the "magic _e_" tells you to use the name of the vowel. Analyze orally before attempting to read the word.

Example: word — <u>joke</u>
"Magic e" makes the vowel say (ō).
The word is <u>joke</u>."

8. Have the child read the following words without any assistance.

joke	lone	rope
side	tale	mere
bone	tile	cave
gale	cake	wipe
vine	mile	vote
poke	case	gaze
here	hole	cube
sake	mute	wove
sale	base	yoke
line	gave	tire
bake	quite	quote
quake	tune	fine
tone	hope	pure
ripe	save	lame
wife	robe	safe
take	mule	home

More "Magic <u>E</u>" Sentences for Dictation and Reading

I like the tone of the tune.
I hope you got a fine tape.
Can you save the lame dog?
<u>His</u> wife made him a fine robe.
It is safe to take the mule home.
A ripe plum will make pure jam.

"Magic <u>E</u>" Words Using Consonant Blends

crate	clove	blaze	grape
skate	stroke	brave	brake
crane	slope	craze	scale
trade	slide	grove	glade
drape	blame	froze	grave
flake	plane	smoke	glaze
plate	blade	prize	stove
spade	scrape	frame	prone
slave	snake	grade	globe
drove			

Sentences for Dictation and Reading

Lift the crate with a crane.
The blade on the skate froze.
It is fun to slide on a wide slope.
The brave men will stop the blaze.
The cake on the stove went up in smoke.
Sam will not trade the prize that Jane gave him.

"Magic <u>E</u>" Words in Which <u>s</u> Has the (z) Sound*

hose	these	chose
nose	pose	wise
fuse	those	close
rise	rose	

Sentences for Dictation and Reading*

Is that a hole in the hose?
<u>John</u> <u>has</u> a red rose.
It is wise to rise on time.

*The <u>s</u> following a long vowel in a base word is usually pronounced (z) for reading, as is the single <u>s</u> at the end of short words like <u>is</u> and <u>his</u>.

REVIEW TESTS USING "MAGIC E" WORDS

The student should be proficient in review tests before continuing to the next step in the sequence. If he is able to read and spell the words in column a easily, continue with the next step in the sequence. If not, take time out to review the preceding materials, and then try column b, etc.

a	b	c	d
save	pile	joke	gave
pole	cube	lone	tire
pile	rake	Jane	bake
vine	name	hide	take
cure	kite	rope	time
crate	lake	skate	poke
vote	crone	robe	tune
poke	mule	side	rope
mope	tide	fire	trade
gaze	tame	tale	fine
drape	wife	hope	ride
tune	tine	same	plate
bite	spade	lime	dine
hole	made	drove	clove
ripe	mire	nine	fate
sake	tone	dame	nape
mute	yule	rule	game
wove	mode	gape	dune
sale	file	tile	zone
base	home	tube	pave

REVIEW TESTS

This review consists of consonant-vowel-consonant and "magic e" words mixed together to check the student's alertness in differentiating between the two.

a	b	c	d
joke	lone	Jane	hid
rope	Kate	rob	side
tale	pole	hope	same
din	mad	nine	dime
win	gap	tile	tub
gale	van	pile	rake
mule	tame	mine	lime
mire	gate	tin	home
fin	duke	save	hat
wipe	tone	rip	line
hole	sale	base	time
life	zone	quit	mop
sole	wade	wake	fume
five	lane	tap	take
nap	not	lane	wore
wave	size	pure	mat
safe	tore	ape	wide
mat	bone	dome	make
gave	tire	bake	rat
time	pal	date	pan
hire	ride	dive	hive

DETACHED SYLLABLE "MAGIC E"

The principle of "magic e" is applied to the reading of syllables taken from actual words. The child is encouraged to spontaneously give a word that contains such a syllable should one occur to him.

Examples	Suggested Words (For Teacher's Use)
lute	absolute
buse	abuse
lude	interlude
bine	combine
sume	consume
bibe	imbibe
trive	contrive
crete	concrete
spire	conspire

The following detached syllables can be given for spelling and reading.

bene	tile	tude	nite
tite	ture	labe	cose
jole	fide	sene	pute
fute	dite	kine	mune
bate	tate	vate	nate
tene	tere	zene	rade
pete	sote	sede	nile
ribe	pede	cate	lene
nize	pere	lade	tize
cade	lide	done	vene
dile	pote	bose	dure
trive	struse	plete	spire
drite	phile	brate	node

TWO-SYLLABLE WORDS CONTAINING "MAGIC E"

in vite	in side	sup pose
es cape	un safe	cos tume
dis like	con fuse	um pire
en close	tad pole	stam pede
dic tate	em pire	en dure
com pete	com pare	con fine
com pote	in hale	un yoke
dis pute	ben zene	ship shape
in vade	mun dane	en tire
in sane	sub lime	im pede
vam pire	man date	bag pipe
en dive	im pure	quag mire
com plete	dis pose*	ad mire
a muse*	ig nore	mis take
im bibe		

Sentences for Dictation and Reading

I will not imbibe impure milk.
It is best not to inhale benzene.
Did the men dislike the umpire?
Do you dislike the costume I made?
We will not dispute that an ape can be cute.
I suppose the men will compete for the job.
It is a mistake to admire a humdrum empire.
Can you dispose of the complete mess?*
Did the umpire amuse the fans?*

*The s following a long vowel in a base word usually has the (z) sound for reading.

 (as in <u>phone</u>)

This is a digraph — that is, two letters together which make one sound.

Phonetic Words for Spelling and Reading

phone	Ralph	graph
Phil	pro phet	pam phlet
el e phant	phrase*	

Phonetic Sentences for Dictation and Reading

A prophet can tell <u>what</u> will happen.
Did you fix the phone to make it ring?
Ralph sent a pamphlet to the entire class.
Can you compare the size of lakes on a graph?

Mnemonic sentence

This sentence can be dramatized. Make a puppet from an old sheet with a magic marker, and tell the following story with these props: a toy elephant, a telephone, a pamphlet, and a graph.

Ralph the prophet gave Phil the elephant a phone,
a pamphlet, and a graph.

*The <u>s</u> following a long vowel in a base word usually has the (z) sound for reading.

CHAPTER VII

INTRODUCING VOWEL DIGRAPHS

The vowel digraphs are introduced in the order of their frequency of use in the language and with consideration of the ease with which they can be learned. Interspersed with the study of vowel digraphs we continue the development and application of syllable division. The student should be proficient in all review lists before beginning these sounds.

The following digraphs are often introduced by simply noting that, "When two vowels go walking, the first one does the talking." This explanation can be sufficient, but a more dramatic presentation, especially to the younger child, will help him remember the concept. For example, "You have been doing so well that today I have decided to teach you eight new sounds — each of which consists of two letters. You know that before a lady and a man get married they have different last names, but, after they get married, they both have the same name — the name of the man. In the sounds you will learn today, the name of the first vowel is the name of the couple." In a classroom situation, the children can role play the "marriage" of the vowel digraphs. Two children walk to the front of the room, each carrying a vowel of the digraph, such as $\boxed{e}$ and $\boxed{a}$. They come back jointly holding a card with $\boxed{ea}$ on it and say, "Our name is (ē)." And so on with each new sound.

After an explanation, show cards with the following digraphs:

ea — oa — ai — ee — ay — oe — [ue — ei for reading only]

The pupil gives the sound of the vowel. This is followed by developing and applying one sound at a time with an identifying key word.

94

We introduce one sound at a time – for instance, ea as in eat. We say, "You are going to spell and read x new words today just by using the sound on this card." Place the card with ea in front of the student and tell him that the words will be purely phonetic and he will use this particular spelling of the sound (ē) wherever he hears it. Give a key word for the sound whenever you refer to it.

When the card is shown to the child as a visual stimulus, he responds to it with the sound only. When the teacher dictates the sound, she identifies the vowel digraph, always using the same key word as: "ea as in eat" "ee as in tree."

PROCEDURE:

1. Dictate the words for spelling.

2. Have the student read the words from cards, tachistoscope or list.

3. Dictate sentences.

4. Have the student read sentences from cards.

REMEMBER:

The card with the sound that is being taught is clearly displayed for reading and spelling.

The vowel digraphs are included in the daily drill of phonic sounds.

When the number of known sound cards becomes quite large, only a portion are reviewed at each lesson. This is done in such a way as to cover them all periodically in a rotating fashion. When a student seems to have mastered a concept, there is a temptation to drop any subsequent work on it. However, intermittent reinforcement is essential to avoid the risk of the skill being forgotten and lost.

MNEMONICS AND HOMONYMS

As many mnemonic devices as can be thought of by the teacher and pupils should be used to help in the spelling. We will give some examples of mnemonic devices but leave others to the creativity of the teacher and the students.

Attention will be brought to homonyms by underlining them. The two sentences containing the homonyms will be grouped together. It is important to have a good memory aid to identify at least one of the homonyms. The other then becomes obvious by the process of elimination.

The following are examples of mnemonic devices that have been developed for spelling in general and homonyms in particular. Mnemonic devices help us, by association, to remember which vowel digraph to use. In the following example we see that, while beach and beech sound alike, they are spelled quite differently. It is important to learn the respective spellings of each homonym.

The beach is by the sea.
I see a beech tree.

Point out that the ($\bar{e}$) in beach and the ($\bar{e}$) in sea make sense together and are spelled the same way. The same is true of the ($\bar{e}$) in beech and the ($\bar{e}$) in tree.

In like manner:

You can eat meat with peas.
I see two people meet.

The drawings below are excellent visual aids to spelling.

DRILL GAME FOR VOWEL DIGRAPHS

Magic Squares*

Children enjoy making words from the "magic squares" which incorporate the new sound that has been learned. With each vowel digraph we have provided a square or two. They can be used as follows:

1. Start in any letter box and move on from one letter to another to make a word. Horizontal, vertical, and diagonal moves are permitted.
2. Do not jump over any letter.
3. A letter from any box may be doubled.

Scoring

Three points for each three-letter word
Four points for each four-letter word
Five points for each five-letter word — and so on. . .

He may earn two bonus points for each additional word he can think of that contains the vowel digraph on the particular magic square. These words need not be made up of the other letters on the square.

*Adapted from Magic Squares by Sally Childs and Ralph de S. Childs (Cambridge: Educators Publishing Service, Inc., 1965).

 **ea** (as in <u>ea</u>t)

Place the card with the vowel digraph <u>ea</u> in front of the child and indicate that all the words in the list to be dictated are purely phonetic and use this spelling of the sound (ē).

Phonetic Words for Spelling and Reading

eat	real	leap	speak
ear	hear	seam	streak
each	bead	bean	sneak
mean	read	reap	squeak
dear	leak	reach	steam
leaf	beak	teach	dream
weak	peak	peach	cream
year	heal	beach	treat
seat	meal	wheat	beast
east	lean	clear	feast
team	heap	clean	yeast
meat	tear	cheap	least

Mnemonics

We point out that the following "wet" words use the <u>ea</u> spelling of (ē).

s <u>ea</u>	t <u>ea</u>	t <u>ea</u> r	b <u>ea</u> c h
s t <u>ea</u> m	s t r <u>ea</u> m	l <u>ea</u> k	p <u>ea</u> c h
			c r <u>ea</u> m

Homonyms

He likes to drink w<u>ea</u>k t<u>ea</u>.
We n<u>ee</u>d seven days in a w<u>ee</u>k.

We b<u>ea</u>t that t<u>ea</u>m.
F<u>ee</u>d him a b<u>ee</u>t.

Mnemonic Sentences

I can h e a r with a c l e a n e a r. (Note the word ear in hear.)
E a c h y e a r we b e a t that t e a m.

The sentences used in dictation can also add to the association of ideas which will facilitate the memorization of the spelling words.

Phonetic Sentences for Dictation and Reading

I like meat and peas.
Do you like weak tea?
Sit on the seat and read.
A clean peach is a treat to eat.
The east beach is near the sea.
We had tea on the beach by the sea.
Did you hear Jan teach Jane to read?
A cheap dress can have a weak seam.
Will had a pea and a bean and a peach for a meal.

Magic Squares

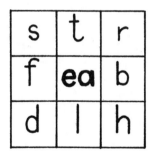
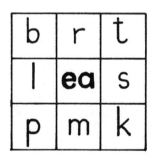

s	t	r
f	ea	b
d	l	h

b	r	t
l	ea	s
p	m	k

t	r	i
s	ea	m
f	a	n

Words which can be formed from the square on the left include:

beat	eat	heal	beast
east	ear	leaf	feast
seal	tea	bead	steal
fear	feat	lead	treat

99

 **oa** (as in s<u>oa</u>p)

This vowel digraph is usually used at the beginning or in the middle of a word.

Phonetic Words for Spelling and Reading

oat	goat	goal	croak
oak	coat	coal	float
loaf	soak	soap	toast
roam	moan	goad	coast
boat	foam	groan	boast
road	toad	cloak	throat
load	loan		

Homonyms

A l<u>oa</u>n is hard to get.
The l<u>o</u>n<u>e</u> puppy cried.

This r<u>oa</u>d has many holes.
He r<u>o</u>d<u>e</u> all day to get here.

Mnemonic Sentences

We l<u>oa</u>d c<u>oa</u>l.
A b<u>oa</u>t can fl<u>oa</u>t.
The b<u>oa</u>t is near the c<u>oa</u>st.
S<u>oa</u>p can fl<u>oa</u>t and make f<u>oa</u>m.

Phonetic Sentences for Dictation and Reading

Can a goat croak?
The boat is made of oak.
Do not roam on the road.
I can hear the toad moan.
Load the oak on the boat.
I can make the goat groan.
He left the boat on the beach.
You can soak the coat in the foam from the soap.

Magic Squares

l	s	d
r	oa	k
g	t	n

c	t	b
s	oa	a
p	g	l

c	t	a
oa	g	b
l	r	o

ai (as in m<u>ai</u>l)

This vowel digraph is usually used at the beginning or in the middle of a word rather than at the end.

Phonetic Words for Spelling and Reading

ail	jail	chain	plain
aid	mail	braid	slain
aim	nail	snail	stain
air	pail	trail	strain
paid	tail	claim	sprain
maid	hail	drain	paint
fail	quail	brain	saint
bail	pain	grain	taint
rail	rain	train	quaint

Homonyms

The m<u>a</u>l<u>e</u> pup was in the m<u>ai</u>l box.

P<u>a</u>l<u>e</u> pink ink was in the red p<u>ai</u>l.

It is a p<u>ai</u>n to clean glass p<u>a</u>n<u>e</u>s.

You must get b<u>ai</u>l to keep out of jail.
This b<u>a</u>l<u>e</u> of hay is wet.

The t<u>a</u>l<u>e</u> was about a pup with a
long t<u>ai</u>l.

Will all that candy <u>ai</u>l you?
<u>A</u>l<u>e</u> is a drink.

102

Phonetic Sentences for Dictation and Reading

A snail <u>has</u> <u>no</u> tail.
When it rains, it can hail.
Do not fail to paint the pail.
It pains <u>me</u> to step on a nail.
The maid paid for the braid.
If you go to jail, you will wail.
A strain and a sprain can pain.
The maid <u>put</u> the hat in the pail.

Magic Squares

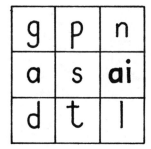

g	p	n
a	s	ai
d	t	l

m	ai	l
r	o	d
b	g	t

 **ee** (as in <u>tree</u>)

Phonetic Words for Spelling and Reading

see	weed	meet	screech
fee	feet	deer	greed
eel	beet	keep	screen
bee	peek	jeep	queen
wee	feed	need	green
heed	peel	flee	steep
peep	seen	tree	sweep
feel	seem	bleed	street
seed	deep	beech	fleet
week	heel	speech	greet
reef			

Homonyms

We m<u>ee</u>t each week.
M<u>ea</u>t is good to eat.

I see a b<u>ee</u>ch tree.
The b<u>ea</u>ch is near the sea.

We have two f<u>ee</u>t.
That trick is a neat f<u>ea</u>t.

The h<u>ee</u>l of his foot hurt.
The doctor can h<u>ea</u>l it.

Mnemonic Sentences

If you p<u>ee</u>k, you can s<u>ee</u>.
You have two f<u>ee</u>t and a h<u>ee</u>l on each.
We m<u>ee</u>t each w<u>ee</u>k.

Phonetic Sentences for Dictation and Reading

I need to keep the jeep.
Did you meet the wee deer?
I can feel the bite of the bee.
Can you peek and not be seen?
You can plant beets <u>from</u> seed.
I see that the queen gave a long speech.

Magic Squares

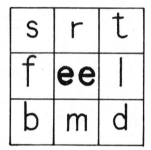

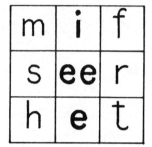

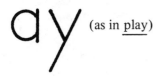 **(as in <u>play</u>)**

"The letter <u>y</u> seems to have a tail. The tail is always at the end of a dog, and <u>ay</u> is usually at the end of a word."

Phonetic Words for Spelling and Reading

gay	may	gray	stray
jay	hay	play	subway
bay	say	stay	Sunday
day	lay	tray	playtime
way	fray	bray	maypole
ray	sway	pray	playmate
pay	clay		

Phonetic Sentences for Dictation and Reading

You may stay and play.
Pay the man for the clay.
The hay will sway in the wind.
<u>We</u> must pay to take the subway.
The ray of the sun makes the day gay.

Magic Squares

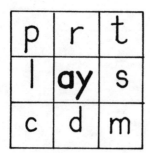

 **oe** (as in t<u>oe</u>)

"The t<u>oe</u> is at the end of the body, and <u>oe</u> is usually at the end of a word."

Phonetic Words for Spelling and Reading

toe	foe	Moe	doeskin
woe	doe	roe	hoecake
hoe	Joe	tiptoe	toenail

Phonetic Sentences for Dictation and Reading

Woe to the foe.
Did Joe stub <u>his</u> toe?
Moe weeds <u>with</u> a hoe.
The <u>egg</u> of the fish is the roe.
You <u>can</u> bake a hoecake on a hoe.
If you stand on tiptoe, you will see the men.

Magic Squares

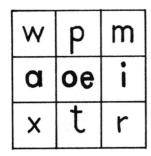

 (as in <u>rescue</u>)   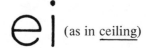 (as in <u>ceiling</u>)

These vowel digraphs were introduced as part of the eight special vowel digraphs, but, since they are found in words that are too difficult for a student's early vocabulary, they are not presented at this time with words and sentences. They are, however, included in the daily drill of the sounds so that the student might become familiar with them.

SYLLABLE DIVISION

Now that the student can read two-syllable words that have been divided for him, we teach him to do this for himself. We tell him that the spelling and reading of a long word can be made easy if we know how to divide it into two simple syllables. One syllable is read at a time and then the whole word is easily put together.

The student is given a mimeographed sheet with a list of two-syllable words. He is taught to divide the words into two syllables using Method I. When this skill is perfected, we progress to Methods II and III, respectively.

METHOD I

Direct the student to:

1. Underline the vowels in red.
2. When two consonants appear between the vowels, split the consonants with a red pencil, or cut them apart with scissors.
3. Read the first syllable, the second syllable and, lastly, the word.
4. Continue until this can be done with facility.

Apply the above method to words from lists a, b, c and d in that order.

a	b	c	d
bonnet	hobnob	subject	combine
muffin	pulpit	pigment	compete
rabbit	tablet	tempest	mundane
tennis	fungus	tandem	sublime
bobbin	humbug	suspect	inhale

METHOD II

Direct the student to:

1. Find vowels but do not underline them.
2. Split consonants with a red pencil.
3. Read the words.

Apply the above method to words from lists a, b, c and d in that order.

a	b	c	d
commit	public	pigment	benzene
pollen	magnet	consent	stampede
happen	peplum	contest	mandate
kitten	helmet	engulf	pancake
fossil	nutmeg	combust	dispute

METHOD III

When the above skill is mastered, direct the student to:

1. Find vowels without underlining them.
2. Split consonants without marking them. Use the "rule of thumb."

> Show how easy it is to read a two-syllable word if you use the "rule of thumb." — <u>Cover the second syllable with your thumb.</u> <u>Read the first syllable, and then read the whole word.</u>

3. Read the word.

Apply the above method to words from lists a, b, c and d in that order.

a	b	c	d
rattan	tandem	consent	vampire
suffix	picnic	dentist	bagpipe
sudden	sampan	splendid	quagmire
gossip	victim	suspend	dictate
bobbin	napkin	disrupt	suppose

Sentences for Reading Only

A game of tennis can be fun.
Did the gossip insult the men?
The rabbit did not like to sniff the pollen.
I <u>have</u> a red velvet ribbon for the bonnet.

Sentences for Dictation and Reading

Did you inquire <u>about</u> the mistake?
<u>We</u> will not dispute that an ape can be cute.
The bandit hid the gun near the banyan tree.
Each year Jim wins the public pancake contest.
It is a mistake not to see the dentist each year.
It will be a problem to make a strong bandstand.
If you stand on tiptoe, you will see the empress.

REVIEW TESTS

TWO-SYLLABLE WORDS

The student should be proficient in review tests before continuing to the next step in the sequence. If he is able to read and spell the words in column a easily, continue with the next step in the sequence. If not, take time out to review the preceding materials, and then try column b, etc.

a	b	c	d
tonsil	unyoke	dispel	vampire
bodkin	despot	dispute	inquire
pancake	empire	imbibe	athlete
intone	tennis	velvet	dislike
goblin	helmet	tantrum	rabbit
goblet	encamp	dragnet	rostrum
pippin	gossip	public	ignite
inflict	submit	tidbit	fossil
stampede	litmus	endive	banyan
bandit	subtract	rumpus	tempest
pigment	neptune	wombat	magnet
benzene	ignite	mundane	concrete
flotsam	mistake	tadpole	cactus
consent	dentist	sampan	empire
combine	lintel	droplet	bagpipe
pepsin	napkin	hobnob	inhale
complete	ramrod	tandem	combust
impure	insult	engulf	contest
solvent	pulpit	umpire	quagmire
fungus	inspect	limpet	

er (as in her)   ir (as in bird)   ur (as in burn)

These are introduced as <u>the three (ər)'s</u>. Place the three cards together in front of the student and explain that all have the same sound,· (ər). After this introduction, develop the patterns one at a time on separate days.

er (as in her)

The spelling e̅r̅ is the most frequently used of the <u>three (ər)'s</u> and should be used as first choice when making an educated guess.

Dictate the Following Words for Spelling and Then Have the Pupil Read Them

fern	perch	timber	hermit
term	stern	silver	Herbert
jerk	under	permit	thunder
her	sister	perhaps	sifter
serf	whisper	shelter	singer
verb	winter	whisker	finger
herd	temper	lantern	linger
Bert	master	tender	monster
perk	number	enter	hunter
pert			

Sentences for Dictation and Reading

<u>He</u> is a stern master.
Perhaps it will thunder.
<u>My</u> sister is under the fern.
<u>He</u> <u>has</u> tender silver whiskers.
The hunter <u>has</u> a winter shelter.
Whisper the number when you enter.
Did Herbert smash <u>his</u> finger with the timber?
If you get the hermit a lantern, <u>he</u> will help you dig.

Words for Reading Only

verse	miller	summer	flutter
terse	hammer	sleeper	teacher
better	dinner	bitter	clerk
deeper	painter	upper	nerve

Sentences for Reading Only

The painter can do a better job.
Did you invite the teacher to dinner?
You must plant the tree a bit deeper.
I hope to see <u>Mr</u>. Miller this summer.

Magic Squares

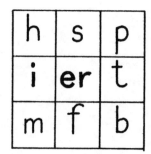

ir  (as in <u>bird</u>)

This is the second most commonly used of the three (ər) sounds. The <u>ir</u>, as in <u>bird</u>, has a dotted <u>i</u>. A bird has a dotted <u>i</u> too.

Dictate the Following Words and Then
Have The Pupil Read Them

sir	stir	whirl	thirst
fir	birch	first	squirm
bird	chirp	skirt	squirt
firm	shirt	smirk	skirmish
dirt	third	swirl	confirm
girl	birth	twirl	birthday

Homonyms

The cat gave <u>birth</u> to three kittens.
He will sleep in the upper <u>berth</u>.

Mnemonic Sentences

A <u>girl</u> can wh<u>ir</u>l in a sk<u>ir</u>t and sh<u>ir</u>t.
A b<u>ir</u>d can ch<u>ir</u>p in a f<u>ir</u> tree.

Sentences for Dictation and Reading

The bird likes to chirp.
The girl likes her red skirt.
Tell him to confirm the date of birth.
The glob of dirt made the girl squirm.
The girl in the red shirt is third in line.

Magic Squares

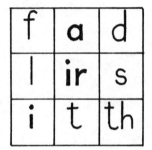

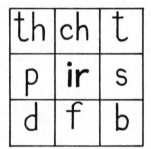

ur (as in <u>burn</u>)

The last thing we want is to burn. <u>Ur</u>, as in <u>burn</u>, is the least commonly used of the three (ər)'s and our last choice.

Words for Spelling and Reading

cur	hurt	curl	urchin
fur	purl	churn	furnish
blur	lurk	church	disturb
burn	hurl	Turk	Saturn
turn	spur	blurt	surplus
curb	slur	burst	

Homonyms

She wore her f<u>ur</u> to the party.
The bird is in the f<u>ir</u> tree.

Sentences for Dictation and Reading

I can hurl the stone.
Do not let the fur burn.
Do not burn the church.
The men will furnish the church.
Tim <u>was</u> hurt when the churn burst.

Mnemonic Story for Reading

Hot Turkey Soup

On Thursday and Saturday we slurp soup. It can curl the hair. It can churn the stomach. It can blur the eyes. It can make you hurt. It can make you burp. If you eat too much, it can make you burst. It can make you so mad that you hurl it.

—contributed by Sue MacDonald

Words for Reading Only

further	murder	Thursday
curve	purse	nurse
Saturday		

Sentences for Reading Only

Do not disturb us on Saturday.
The name of the planet is Saturn.
The bottom of the purse had a curve.
He did not blur the surface of the glass.
I will see the nurse on Thursday.
Thursday and Saturday are the names of days of the week.

Magic Squares

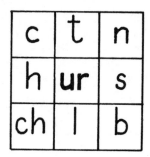

OW (as in <u>clown</u>)   OU (as in <u>ouch</u>)

The above sounds are taught together as the <u>two</u> (o u)'s.

OW (as in <u>clown</u>)

This one is taught first. Remember to display the card with the sound being taught in front of the student while related words and sentences are read and spelled.

Words for Spelling and Reading

owl	howl	plow	crown
bow	down	scowl	brown
how	town	growl	drown
cow	gown	clown	crowd
now	brow	frown	prowl
fowl			

Sentences for Dictation and Reading

Is an owl a fowl?
A clown can frown for fun.
The crowd went downtown.
<u>She</u> had a brown velvet gown.
The dog will growl if you scowl.
How now brown cow?

Words for Reading Only

power	tower	powder	towel
shower	vowel	flower	prowler

Sentences for Reading Only

The dog will howl at the prowler.
It is fun to make a tower in the sand.
Wipe the powder <u>off</u> the shelf with a towel.

Magic Squares

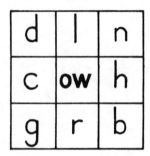

120

OU (as in <u>ouch</u>)

We say, "If I pinch you (demonstrate gently), you will say 'ouch.' If I pinch a piece off the <u>o w</u>, it will become <u>o u</u>."

Words for Spelling and Reading

out	south	shout	pound
our	slouch	grouch	round
ouch	proud	crouch	sound
couch	scout	cloud	count
pouch	scour	stout	mount
loud	flour	snout	hound
sour	spout	bound	wound
pout	trout	found	ground
mouth	sprout	mound	

Sentences for Dictation and Reading

We fish for trout in the south.
A loud sound came <u>from</u> the spout.
Make a round mound on the ground.
You can pound the wheat to get flour.
Tim will slouch if he sits on our couch.

Words for Reading Only

thousand   mouse   house   blouse

Sentences for Reading Only

<u>Dot</u> left her blouse on the couch.
The scout found a thousand bags of flour.
A mouse in the house will make Mom shout.

Magic Squares

s	t	e
ou	h	a
m	r	g

 **(as in <u>light</u>)**

"Today we are going to learn three letters that make one sound — (igh) as in <u>light</u>." Pointing to the light in the room becomes the signal for the sound.

Words for Spelling and Reading

nigh	fight	right	flight
sigh	might	tight	plight
high	light	fright	slight
sight	night	bright	blight

Sentences for Dictation and Reading

Is the light <u>off</u> at night?
The rope is <u>high</u> and tight.
I sigh at the sight of a fight.
He might sight the bright light.

Words for Reading Only

brighten	frighten	insight
affright	lighten	limelight

Sentences for Reading Only

The dog might frighten the cat.
Can you brighten the light with a better bulb?
You will lighten the load if you leave the trunk at home.

SYLLABLE ENDINGS: <u>ble</u> – <u>fle</u> – <u>tle</u> – <u>dle</u> – <u>gle</u> – <u>kle</u> – <u>ple</u> – <u>zle</u>

To facilitate the decoding of a word, these common endings can be cut off and the rest of the word can then be read more easily. The above endings are presented, each one on a separate card, with a related word on the reverse side. The pupil does not use these as key words. He will merely read the sound and its word.

Example:

ble – stumble
fle – sniffle
tle – battle
dle – handle
gle – jungle
kle – rankle
ple – simple
zle – dazzle

Present the endings <u>ble</u>, <u>fle</u>, <u>tle</u>, <u>dle</u>, <u>gle</u>, <u>kle</u>, <u>ple</u> and <u>zle</u>, each on a separate card. Keep the cards with the endings clearly displayed in front of the student while the work is being done.

Using the following list of words, have the student:

1. Cut off the ending with a red pencil or with the "rule of thumb."
2. Read the first syllable.
3. Read the word.

handle	simple	ramble	nimble
bundle	sample	bumble	tangle
humble	dimple	rankle	jungle
rumble	fondle	fumble	bungle
jumble	candle	gamble	tumble
ankle	grumble	tremble	spindle
stumble	crumble		

The following list is phonetic for spelling and reading with the application of the "rule of twins." (Whenever a letter is doubled, we call it "twins.")

"When these endings follow a short vowel sound, the first letter of the ending is usually doubled."

muddle	giggle	bottle	fizzle
apple	cuddle	wiggle	waggle
riddle	pebble	muffle	juggle
settle	cattle	battle	fiddle
ruffle	dazzle	saddle	kettle
middle	paddle	meddle	hobble
little	sizzle	guzzle	tattle
cripple	prattle	drizzle	grizzle
bubble			

Phonetic Sentences for Dictation and Reading

I rankle at a battle in the saddle.
The pebble made the cattle tremble.
Can you juggle an apple and a pebble?
The bubble made a rumble in the kettle.
A snake can wiggle and waggle in the jungle.
The man with the fiddle had to muffle his giggle.
I like to fondle the ruffle in the middle of a dress.

Spelling Drill Exercise

The following list can be mimeographed for additional practice.

<u>Twins</u> or <u>Not Twins</u>?

Spell the word correctly on the blank lines.

1. mi   dle _____
2. bo   tle _____
3. gam   ble _____
4. li   tle _____
5. gi   gle _____
6. wi   gle _____
7. sa   dle _____

8. star tle _____
9. an   kle _____
10. se   tle _____
11. sni fle _____
12. can dle _____
13. rum ble _____

WORDS ENDING IN <u>ild</u> – <u>old</u> – <u>ind</u> – <u>ost</u> – <u>olt</u>

A few word "families" have a long vowel sound before a final blend. These are best learned as special patterns.

Words for Spelling and Reading

<u>ild</u>	<u>old</u>	<u>ind</u>	<u>olt</u>	<u>ost</u>
child	cold	bind	bolt	most
mild	bold	blind	colt	host
wild	fold	find	jolt	post
	gold	grind	volt	almost
	hold	hind		hostess
	mold	kind		
	sold	mind		
	scold	rind		
	told	wind		
	old	behind		
		remind		

Sentences for Dictation and Reading

A wild child is not mild.
A child that minds is not bad.
The bold old man sold the gold.
A colt may bolt if you scold him.
The host and hostess were almost late.

ar (as in <u>star</u>)

Phonetic Words for Spelling and Reading

art	card	barb	scarf
arm	tart	yard	garlic
ark	hard	chart	tarnish
bar	carp	charm	marlin
car	bark	parch	artist
tar	dark	march	bombard
far	darn	shark	target
jar	part	sharp	discard
arch	lard	harsh	harmless
star	mark	marsh	startle
scar	park	snarl	marble
spar	lark	spark	sparkle
harp	farm	start	gargle
cart	harm	smart	garble
barn	yarn	stark	
dart			

Phonetic Sentences for Dictation and Reading

That is a sharp dart.
You can go far in a car.
Do not park in the dark.
A star shines in the dark.
White marble can sparkle.
We mend and darn with yarn.
The artist charms us with his art.
The cart is in the barn on the farm.

Poem

Twinkle, twinkle little star,
How I wonder what you are,
Up above the sky so high,
Like a diamond in the sky.

Words for Reading Only

starve	harness	partner	starter
sharpen	carbon	marvel	harden
garden	harvest	garment	market

Sentences for Reading Only

He left the garments on the bar.
Do not startle the lark in the garden.
We may starve if you do not <u>work</u> in the garden.

Magic Squares

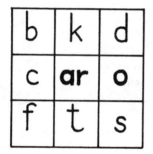

or (as in <u>horn</u>)

Phonetic Words for Spelling and Reading

or	morn	torch	storm	morbid
for	sort	thorn	stork	orbit
nor	fork	north	scorn	forlorn
cord	pork	short	sport	forget
form	horn	shorn	snort	forgave
born	lord	porch	sworn	sordid
corn	worn	forth	scorch	northwest

Phonetic Sentences for Dictation and Reading

Do not scorch the corn.
A stork <u>was</u> born in the morn.
The storm came from the north.
If you forget <u>me</u>, I will be forlorn.
It is a thrill to think of men in orbit.

Words for Reading Only

order	corner	normal	horse	northern
morsel	border	cork	hornet	mortal

Sentences for Reading Only

Did you order the cord?
The border is made of cork.
I do not like the sting of a hornet.
He gave <u>me</u> just a morsel of cake.

Magic Squares

t	s	f
h	or	e
b	m	n

c	k	m
f	or	d
t	p	n

129

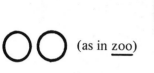 (as in <u>zoo</u>)

"We have animals with two big round eyes in the ZOO."

Words for Spelling and Reading

too	room	spool	igloo
coo	boom	bloom	boost
zoo	soon	gloom	roost
coop	hoop	spoon	poodle
mood	hoot	droop	harpoon
moon	shoot	stoop	lampoon
roof	booth	broom	cartoon
cool	proof	scoop	mushroom
loop	stool	brood	baboon
pool	swoop		

Sentences for Dictation and Reading

It is cool in the pool.
The plant is on the stool.
The igloo had a big room.
Loop the twine on a hoop.
Did the men land on the moon?
The poodle got on the roof at the zoo.

Sentences for Reading Only

Which <u>school</u> did you choose?
I need a <u>bootie</u> for the papoose.
Can a rooster lay an <u>egg</u>?

Magic Squares

 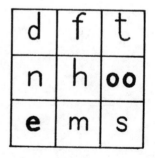

ENDINGS: <u>ly</u> – <u>vy</u> – <u>by</u> – <u>dy</u> – <u>ty</u> – <u>fy</u> – <u>ny</u> – <u>py</u> – <u>sy</u>

The above endings are presented, each on a separate card, with a related word on the other side. When reviewing the sound pack, the pupil reads the sound and its word.

ly – manly
vy – envy
by – hobby
dy – windy
ty – rusty
fy – stuffy
ny – penny
py – puppy
sy – patsy

Keep the cards with the endings clearly displayed in front of the student while dictating words for spelling.

For reading, have the student:

1. Cut off the ending with a red pencil or with the "rule of thumb."
2. Read the first syllable.
3. Read the word.

Phonetic Words for Spelling and Reading

windy	manly	crusty	ninety
dusty	runty	grumpy	stately
rusty	fifty	frisky	dandy
Randy	misty	crispy	handy
madly	dusky	sixty	party
candy	chunky	sandy	

Words for Reading Only

fairy	forty	lately	beastly
twenty	rainy	sweetly	nearly
story	thirty	deeply	

The following list is phonetic for spelling and reading with the application of the "rule of twins."

"When these endings follow a short vowel sound, the first letter of the ending is usually doubled."

muddy	snuffy	caddy	daddy
stubby	penny	Benny	happy
funny	berry	witty	snappy
mommy	hobby	Betty	puppy
sloppy	hurry	Sammy	

Spelling Drill Exercise

The following list may be mimeographed for additional practice.

Twins or Not Twins?
Spell the word correctly on the blank lines.

1. dus   ty   ——————   7.   nin   ty   ——————

2. pe   ny   ——————   8.   fu   ny   ——————

3. pu   py   ——————   9.   mu   dy   ——————

4. state   ly   ——————   10.   mo   my   ——————

5. hu   ry   ——————   11.   be   ry   ——————

6. dan   dy   ——————   12.   par   ty   ——————

Phonetic Sentences for Dictation and Reading

I like a frisky puppy.
Patsy had a penny candy.
A man of ninety can be grumpy.
A witty girl can make funny jokes.
Sammy made crispy, chunky candy.
This shelf gets dusty when it is windy.
A rusty shelf can make a hobby sloppy.

FOR OLDER CHILDREN

Introduce **ly** as a suffix and define **suffix**.

Suffix — A syllable added to the end of a word that will change its meaning and
form a new word.

The suffix **ly** often means "in a certain way."

Example: fondly — in a fond way
              safely — in a safe way

An adjective becomes an adverb when **ly** is added.

sad — sadly	grim — grimly
bad — badly	grand — grandly
trim — trimly	limp — limply
fond — fondly	late — lately
dim — dimly	crisp — crisply
glad — gladly	close — closely
grave — gravely	safe — safely
tame — tamely	

Exception: How to Spell (kē) — ky or key

The following mnemonic riddles may be put on a card.

What kind of key can you eat?   (a turkey)
What kind of key can kick?   (a donkey)
What kind of key can climb a tree? (a monkey)
What kind of key is a game?   (hockey)

Here is the key to help you remember.

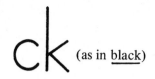 (as in <u>black</u>)

<u>C</u> and <u>k</u> say (ck) separately and together. When they are together, as in <u>black</u>, they are usually at the end of a word. They never appear together at the beginning of a word.

When you hear the (k) sound after a short vowel in a one-syllable word, it is usually spelled with <u>ck</u>.

Phonetic Words for Spelling and Reading

tack	rack	quick	block
back	dock	chuck	cluck
sack	buck	crack	clock
sock	luck	truck	struck
sick	duck	track	pocket
hack	puck	trick	docket
tick	suck	crock	rocker
lick	quack	smack	cracker
Jack	chick	mock	tick-tock
pick	shack	click	bucket
pack	snack	black	

Phonetic Sentences for Dictation and Reading

Send the sack back.
Quick, get <u>off</u> the truck!
Did the cat lick the chick?
Can you hear the clock tick?
Get the sack back on the truck.
The clock in the shack struck ten.
The duck will quack to get a snack.
The black sock will <u>match</u> the stripes on the dress.

Poem

Jack be nimble
Jack be quick
Jack jump over
the candle stick.

134

REMEMBER

When you hear the (k) sound at the end of a word, it is spelled with a k̲:

1. When preceded by a vowel that says its name (long vowel followed by a consonant and "magic e̲").

lake   make   sake   poke

2. When preceded by a double vowel (vowel digraph).

look   sneak   croak   cook

3. When preceded by a consonant.

bank   clank   honk   hunk

After a vowel that says its name, such as in "magic e̲" words, the (k) sound is spelled with a k̲.

rake	like	wake
take	lake	flake
snake	make	shake
spoke	sake	woke
spike	fake	poke
strike	bake	stake
Jake	brake	dike
Mike	cake	yoke
pike	drake	joke
hike		

HARD – SOFT C

Review c as a hard sound in the initial position.

can	class	crib	came
cap	cliff	crash	cave
cup	clap	camp	card
cut	club	clamp	cone
cub	clam	crust	canteen
cud	clod	cane	carpet
cog	clip	cape	candy
cash			

Sentences for Dictation

I like corn on the cob.
The cat slept in the crib.
The club had a canteen at the camp.
The cup fell on the carpet with a crash.

Place a chart with the letters e, i and y in a conspicuous position. Then, take the following cards ca, co, cu, cr, cl, ci, ce and cy. Tell the child that, as each of the cards is flashed to him, he should say (k) in response to the initial consonant except when the c is followed by e, i or y and then he should say, "CHANGE." This is drilled until he can do it without referring to the clues on the chart.

The above exercise provides the student with a rule that serves as a signal to "CHANGE" the sound of c from hard to soft. We tell him that the c "CHANGES" to the sound (s) when followed by e, i or y.

Now when the cards are flashed, he should say (k) or (s) as the case may be.

Soft c Words for Spelling and Reading

cent	place	mice	citrus
cinch	race	brace	pencil
cell	trace	thrice	fancy
ice	nice	ulcer	except
ace	mace	center	Nancy
face	rice	cinder	advice
lace	certain	space	
circus	twice		

136

Soft c Words for Reading Only

quince	cease	circle	citron
census	fleece	fence	trance
lance	prince	spice	space

Sentences for Dictation and Reading

Indicate that all the (s) sounds in these sentences will be spelled with c.

I like a nice pencil.
Nancy fell on the ice twice.
Mice are nice but not in rice.
Is it a cinch to win the race?
My advice is to clean the place.

SUMMARY

C is usually pronounced as (k) except when it is followed by e, i or y, and then it is pronounced as (s).

In the beginning of a word, the (k) sound is usually spelled with a c, except when it is followed by e, i or y, and then a k is used.

Example: key   kit   cat   can   cot

The following drill can be used for this rule:

Fill in the blank with c or k.
Remember that c is pronounced as (k)
when followed by anything except e, i or y.

_____ eep	_____ ind
_____ ute	_____ iln
_____ one	_____ art
_____ all	_____ ar
_____ lear	_____ eel
_____ ure	_____ in
_____ ome	_____ een
_____ ing	_____ oat
_____ ick	_____ oal
_____ ut	_____ are
_____ ub	_____ ode
_____ ave	_____ rib

137

Use card drill for hard and soft c again and explain that the words that follow have both hard and soft c included.

cent	scrape	crept	lace
price	scrub	ice	advice
twice	crisp	rice	rancid
cancel	nice	center	crib
costume	slice	campus	crush
cramp	brace	crust	crunch
fence	crane	trace	space
cell	mice	cinder	pencil
talcum	excite	face	place
scant	crimp	grace	

Sentences for Dictation and Reading

All the (s) sounds are spelled with c.

What is the price of the fence?
Tell Grace to fill the cup twice.
He had to cancel the trip to camp.
I can crush the clove with a fork.
The club will get ten white mice.

HARD – SOFT G

Review g as a hard sound in the initial position.

got	grin	gosh	globe
gat	glad	gulf	glide
gob	grab	gate	glass
gum	glen	game	grill
gun	grip	gave	grave
Gus	grit	gale	grape
gull	gust		

Sentences for Dictation and Reading

I got a globe as a gift.
I got a big gob of gum.
I gave the glass to Glen.
He gave the man some gas.*
Gwen will play next to the gate.
A gust of wind will help him glide.

Display a chart with the letters e, i and y. Then, take the following cards from the case: ga, ge, gi, gl, go, gr, gu and gy. Tell the child that as each of the cards is flashed to him, he should say (g) except when the g is followed by e, i or y, and then he should say "CHANGE." Drill until he can do this without referring to the chart.

Next, tell him that the sound it changes to is (j). When the cards are now flashed, he should say (g) or (j) as the case may be.

Soft g Words for Spelling and Reading

gem	age	magic	ginger
rage	stage	congest	gentle
page	wage	margin	Roger
cage	huge		

*Gas is an exception to the s/z rule for single s at the end of short words.

139

Sentences for Dictation and Reading

I like ginger in cake.
Roger left his pet in the cage.
Magic made the page seem huge.
He did not tell the age of the gem.

Words for Reading Only

cringe	serge	strange	exchange
binge	singe	urgent	indulge
urge	charge	manage	gesture
germ	range	vantage	

Sentence for Reading Only

How did you manage to make that strange gesture?

SUMMARY

G is usually pronounced as (g) as in go, except when it is followed by e, i or y and then it is pronounced as (j).

When you hear the sound (j), it is usually spelled with a g if it is followed by e, i or y.

The following spelling drill can be used for this rule:

The blanks in the following words all have the sound (j). Fill in the blank with g or j according to the rule just learned.

____elatin	____oust
____umper	ori____in
pa____e	bar____e
____ail	____oke
ca____e	con____est
ener____etic	____ab
____am	____ade
mar____in	____entle
____ob	____ack
hu____e	ra____e
____unk	____ungle
____ust	wa____e

Use card drill for hard and soft g again and explain that the words that follow have both hard and soft g included.

glad	margin	gust	gulf
gem	grab	gull	grip
Glen	Gale	Roger	game
rage	gosh	congest	globe
gate	huge	grave	stage
page	grill	glob	gave
glass	age	grape	grin
cage	gentle	wage	stingy
ginger			

Sentences for Dictation and Reading

All the (j) sounds are spelled with a g.

I gave a globe to Roger.
He left a glob on the page.
Gale is gentle with her dog.
Do not grab the gem from Glen.
I am glad the gate is on the cage.
Did you play the game on the stage?

GE – DGE

The (j) sound at the end of the word is usually spelled ge or dge.

ge – After a long vowel

cage	rage	page	sage
wage	huge	stage	

ge – When a consonant precedes the (j) sound

barge	large	fringe	plunge
gorge	forge	cringe	range
urge	strange	verge	serge
change			

dge – After a short vowel

ledge	budge	dredge	smudge
edge	badge	lodge	hedge
fudge	ridge	dodge	grudge
trudge	wedge	judge	bridge

Spelling Drill Exercise: ge – dge

The following list may be mimeographed for additional practice.

Fill in the blanks with the correct endings.

ca	_____	pa	_____	we	_____	le	_____
ran	_____	ur	_____	ju	_____	ri	_____
bri	_____	e	_____	bu	_____	lar	_____
fu	_____	hu	_____	bar	_____	stran	_____

Sentences for Dictation and Reading

The huge ape was on the edge of the cliff.
The fudge made a smudge on the page.
Did the judge make the robber cringe?
The bridge had a huge change booth.

REVIEW – FOR READING AND SPELLING

HARD-SOFT C and G

a	b	c	d
gore	crop	cat	race
trace	can	cramp	gum
gun	crisp	crimp	crept
crib	crush	cap	cob
cup	cut	brace	Grace
ice	rice	cub	cake
circus	cane	crust	crest
crunch	gull	Gus	gust
gulf	scrape	scrub	scamp
scat	scale	cape	cave
core	cure	mice	nice
slice	price	glad	glaze
glass	glide	scant	cent
face	center	cube	clam
twice	grand	grate	grape
grip	globe	glade	grade
cell	place	space	clip
clod	clove	crab	grit
grill	grove	age	cage
page	stage	crate	crane
orange	strange	change	hinge

Hard-Soft c and g Sentences for Reading

He ate an ice cream cone.
You must scrub the cut twice.
Lace will be cute on the cape.
I like crisp crusts on grape tarts.
Gus can brace the side of the cave.
The cat will make the mice scamper.
Grace will clamp the glass with a clip.

Y AS A VOWEL

<u>Y</u> is sometimes pronounced as (ī).

The teacher points to her own eyes, draws the word in the following fashion and says, "There are two eyes with a nose in the middle."

This will help them to remember how to spell <u>eye</u>.

Words with <u>y</u> pronounced as (ī)

by	dry	pry	sky
my	spy	thy	style
why	spry	rye	type
try	fly	shy	tyke
cry	fry		

Endings with <u>y</u> pronounced as (ī)

by – lullaby
fy – satisfy – horrify – signify
ny – deny
py – occupy
ly – July – imply – reply

Sentences for Dictation and Spelling

You can type.
<u>She</u> is shy.
Do not cry.
<u>There</u> is a strange cloud in the sky.
Please reply to my letter.

USE OF LONG VOWEL IN SYLLABLE DIVISION

Syllable division, as we have seen, serves as an important technique to permit the student to decode simple words for spelling and reading. It is also an aid in breaking down more complex words into their elements. When each individual syllable can be more easily identified, the student is better equipped to spell and read polysyllabic words.

He has been taught that:

1. A word has as many syllables as it has vowel sounds.
2. When two consonants appear between the vowels, divide between the consonants.

We now introduce words that are divided after a long vowel.

1. Teach the following familiar words by saying that e̲ and o̲ say their name (long vowel sound) at the end of a short word.

he	me	we	she	be
no	so	go	ho	

2. Tell the student that the vowel at the end of a syllable will usually say its name (long vowel sound).

Words are presented with their syllables clearly divided as shown in the following list.

pu pil	ho tel	mo tel	be gan
o mit	be gin	ba sin	ti ger
pi lot	ba sis	re mit	mi nus

Exercise for Syllable Division with Long Vowel Sound

1. Underline the vowels in red.
2. If there is only one consonant between the two vowels, divide in front of the consonant.
3. The vowel at the end of the syllable then says its name (long vowel).

The following list of words is presented to the student on a mimeographed sheet.

Words for Syllable Division

label	unit	Ajax	lilac
open	item	beset	human
zenith	sequel	focus	bonus
totem	topaz	omit	climax
broken	erect	moment	event
depend	silent	refund	secret
decent	demand	defend	rodent
belong	propose	relent	pretend
protect	prevent	program	spoken
tripod	craven	crisis	promote
grocer	agent	tyrant	regard
decode	erase	donate	locate
polite	became	behave	beside
unite	refine	humane	denote
provide	vacate	tirade	recite
brocade			

Story for Reading and/or Dictation

Snoopy

Snoopy is a crazy puppy. He thinks he can make noble sounds on his bugle. I will tell you a secret <u>about</u> his tunes. <u>They</u> can make a lazy lady run and hide. <u>They</u> can make a tiny pony shake. <u>They</u> even make the acorns fall <u>off</u> little oak trees!

—contributed by Carolyn Smith

Review of Endings: ble – fle – dle – gle – ple – tle – kle

These endings are considered syllables in themselves.

Exercise

1. Cut off the ending either with a red pencil or with the "rule of thumb."
2. Read the word.

bugle	table	able	fable
maple	noble	Bible	idle
rifle	sable	title	cable
ladle	stable	ruble	gable
cradle	bridle	staple	trifle
stifle			

To Facilitate Reading

Cutting Off Endings – ly, vy, by, dy, ny, cy, ky and zy

Exercise

1. Cut off the ending either with a red pencil or with the "rule of thumb."
2. Read the word.

baby	pony	lady	tiny
gravy	navy	holy	shady
lazy	zany*	lacy	Brady
Tracy	slimy	shaky	hazy
shaly*			

Sentences for Dictation and Reading

Can you erase the mark the baby made?
Does the pony have a bridle?
Can you keep our secret?
Change the rodent's cage at once!
This table has a lazy Susan in the center.
There is a demand for rice and gravy every Sunday.

*zany – a silly fellow
*shaly – like shale (a type of rock)

147

SYLLABLE REVIEW

Present the following list of words on a mimeographed sheet.

Divide the words with a slash. Then read the words. Some have one consonant between two vowels, and some have two consonants between the vowels.

sampan	tablet
puppy	belong
lady	hazy
bible	table
moment	vampire
pancake	demand
secret	title
unite	baby
pumpkin	pigpen
brocade	droplet
donate	tantrum
tiny	able

 (as in <u>straw</u>)    (as in <u>August</u>)   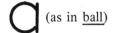 (as in <u>ball</u>)

Teach them as the <u>three (ȯ)'s</u>.

 (as in <u>straw</u>)

This is the spelling for the (o) sound which is often at the end of a word or syllable. A number of words like <u>lawn</u> and <u>shawl</u> have <u>aw</u> in the middle of the word before the letter <u>n</u> or <u>l</u>.

Words for Spelling and Reading

law	flaw	shawl	drawn
paw	straw	dawn	crawl
thaw	squaw	scrawl	tawny
caw	hawk .	drawl	crawfish
jaw	lawn	brawl	dawdle
raw	pawn	sprawl	Hawthorn
claw	bawl	squawk	yawn
draw	awl	prawn*	

Sentences for Dictation and Reading

The hawk had a big claw.
The squaw wore a big shawl.
I like to scrawl when I draw.
He left the straw on the lawn.
I yawn when I get up in the dawn.

Words for Reading Only

seesaw   outlaw   drawer

*prawn—an edible shrimplike animal found in both fresh and salt water

149

Sentences for Reading Only

It is fun to play on a seesaw.
I think the outlaw will not dawdle.

Magic Squares

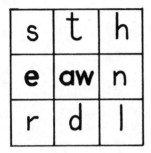

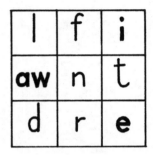

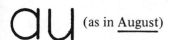 **au** (as in <u>August</u>)

Two of the (o)'s almost look alike—but not quite. When you write the <u>w</u> in <u>aw</u> in a hurry, you forget the bridge and it becomes a <u>u</u>.

Words for Spelling and Reading

haul	daub	gaunt	haunch
Paul	fraud	daunt	launch
Saul	flaunt	haunt	jaunty
taut	fault	vault	audit
maul			

Sentences for Dictation and Reading

Saul is gaunt and ill.
Did the cat maul the dog?
Paul left the cash in the vault.

Words for Reading Only

saunter	laurel	caustic	pauper
author	nautical	pause	saucer
gauze	auto	austere	autumn

Sentences for Reading Only

He is the author of a nautical tale.
A pauper may not <u>have</u> a cup and saucer.
Can you pause and admire the autumn leaves?

Magic Squares

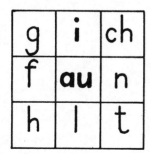

a (as in <u>ball</u>)

The letter <u>a</u> has an (o) sound in a few words. Most of them are words of one syllable in which the <u>a</u> is followed by <u>l</u> or <u>r</u> (<u>call</u>, <u>bald</u>, <u>salt</u>; <u>war</u>, <u>warm</u>).

Words for Dictation and Reading

all	malt	war	walrus
call	warm	walk	walnut
quarter	salt	bald	altar
water	talk		

Sentences for Dictation and Reading

Water, water <u>everywhere</u>, and not a drop to drink.
Call the waiter and ask for a malt.
Is a walnut <u>good</u> when you dip it in salt?

O i (as in <u>oi</u>l)　　　　O y (as in <u>boy</u>)

We introduce <u>oi</u> and <u>oy</u> together. Point out that <u>oi</u> is usually within a word and <u>oy</u> is usually at the end of a word.

O i (as in <u>oi</u>l)

This can be dramatized by having the teacher put both hands on her head, shaking it vigorously and exclaiming, "oi, oi, oi."

Words for Spelling and Reading

oil	coil	quoit*	hoist
toil	coif*	spoil	broil
soil	void	joint	tinfoil
boil	moil*	point	exploit
coin	foil	moist	tabloid
join	loin	joist	

Sentences for Dictation and Reading

Do not boil the oil.
Join the pipe at the joint.
Point at the coin you like.
You must toil to till the soil.
I like to get tinfoil when I broil fish with oil.

*coif　— a close-fitting cap
*moil　— hard work, drudgery; turmoil
*quoit — a flat ring-shaped piece of iron to be pitched at a fixed object in a game
　　　　similar to horseshoes

Words for Reading Only

choice	voice	coinage	moisture
poison	sirloin	anoint	embroider
thyroid	turmoil		

Sentences for Reading Only

Do not speak in a loud voice.
Poison on meat is bad to eat.
I like to eat a choice cut of sirloin.

Magic Squares

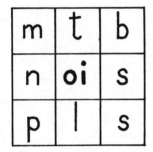 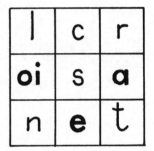

 **oy** (as in <u>boy</u>)

"<u>Y</u> looks like a letter with a tail. A puppy has a tail at the end of him. <u>Oy</u> tends to be found at the end of a word because of the tail on the <u>y</u>."

Words for Spelling and Reading

toy	coy	enjoy	decoy
Roy	soy	envoy	oyster
joy	Troy	employ	convoy
boy	ploy*		

Sentences for Dictation and Reading

The boy will like the toy.
I can go on a trip to Troy.
It is a joy to eat an oyster.
Roy went on a trip with a convoy.

Words for Reading Only

annoy	alloy	loyal	destroy
voyage	boycott	corduroy	flamboyant

Sentences for Reading Only

I <u>would</u> like a corduroy dress.
If you annoy him, he may destroy <u>your</u> toy.
The men on the voyage <u>were</u> loyal to the leader.

Magic Squares

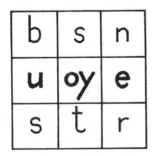

*ploy—a trick or stratagem to outwit an opponent

 **tch** (as in <u>catch</u>)

<u>Tch</u> is a consonant trigraph.
This spelling of the (ch) sound is usually used at the end of the word
following a short vowel.

Words for Spelling and Reading

itch	witch	hutch	scratch
thatch	pitch	blotch	clutch
latch	hitch	crotch	sketch
catch	ditch	stretch	Scotch
hatch	match	stitch	splotch
fetch	botch	crutch	ketchup
Dutch	patch		

Sentences for Dictation and Reading

Can you catch if I pitch?
I must scratch the itch.
Did you catch the witch?
The witch fell in the ditch.
A patch on the skin can itch.
Do not pitch the tent near the ditch.

Words for Reading Only

pitcher	kitchen
satchel	stretcher

Sentences for Reading Only

The pitcher is in the kitchen.
I need a satchel with a strong catch.
The stretcher had a patch in the middle.

SOME ADDITIONAL INFORMATION

1. When a monosyllable ends with the (ch) sound and a short vowel precedes it, it is usually spelled <u>tch</u>.

Example: match   pitch   catch   hatch

The <u>tch</u> spelling also occurs in the middle of a few polysyllabic words such as:

kitchen   pitcher   hatchet   satchel

2. Note these commonly used exceptions and a sentence to help remember them.

   rich   much   which   such

   The <u>rich</u> have <u>much</u> with <u>which</u> to buy <u>such</u> stuff.

Additional exceptions are:

   ostrich   detach   attach   sandwich

3. If anything except a short vowel comes before the final (ch), it is spelled <u>ch</u>.

Example: ouch   inch   branch   bunch
         march   ranch   pinch   starch

4. At the beginning of words, the sound (ch) is spelled <u>ch</u>.

   chin   chop   chat   chill

ING AS AN ENDING

Instruct the student to:

1. Cut off the ending with a red pencil or with the "rule of thumb."
2. Read the first syllable.
3. Read the word.

Words for Spelling and Reading

hashing	messing	dressing	listing
mashing	hissing	pressing	bending
lashing	kissing	staffing	bumping
gashing	fussing	snuffing	camping
wishing	yelling	sniffing	landing
doffing	weeding	smelling	milking
buffing	culling	grilling	resting
puffing	smashing	shrilling	tilting
whiffing	crashing	scuffing	jumping
selling	flashing	classing	fasting
telling	blushing	thrilling	helping
billing	brushing	spilling	grunting
killing	falling	stressing	printing
willing	fishing	risking	trusting
hulling	mocking	mending	stamping
mulling	spelling	handing	drifting
massing	swelling	yelping	planting
mussing	stuffing	dusting	branding
crisping	hanging	dunking	drinking
granting	longing	junking	slinging
plumping	sinking	stinking	stinging
slanting	linking	bringing	swinging
standing	pinking	stringing	plunking
ringing	honking	clanging	clunking
banging	conking	clinking	eating
singing			

158

Sentences for Dictation and Reading

The men are willing to do the billing.
It is not thrilling to see a snake hissing.
He was grunting while helping with the planting.
If we all help with the planting, we can go camping.
We were standing when the bell was ringing and clanging.
A pretty mocking bird was singing in an old oak tree.
Are you wishing to go camping in August?
The little toy duck made a nice loud quacking sound.

Story for Reading and/or Dictation

Hank

Hank was a little stinging bee. Hank was drinking nectar from a flower.

My uncle was weeding the junk out of the garden. He did not see Hank hanging around.

Hank was longing for a bite of meat. He sprang at my uncle.

All of a sudden, my uncle was jumping up and down. My uncle was brushing off his pants. Hank went falling off without eating. My uncle was thankful that he had on long pants!

—contributed by Carolyn Smith

Review Sentences for Dictation and Reading

The large wedge cost sixty cents.
A Sloppy Joe is a messy sandwich.
It is simple to giggle at a funny joke.
The child got stuck on the muddy road.
The quick little sneak was able to steal the candy.
The old man got stuck in the middle of the street.
The witch had a purple broom. Her cat would scratch the middle of his back against the handy broom.

CHAPTER VIII

VOWEL-CONSONANT-VOWEL SPELLING RULE

The rules that follow in this chapter deal with more complex material. The "Vowel-Consonant-Vowel Spelling Rule" requires that the student be aware of both the root word and the suffix before he can decide when to double the final consonant of the root word.

The sounds that are interspersed with the spelling rules are those which are less frequently used. Some of the vowel digraphs are second or third choices to sounds or spellings already taught.

The final section deals with root words and affixes and serves to develop the vocabulary of the older child.

Rule

Short (one-syllable) words that end in a single consonant, preceded by a single vowel, double the final consonant when adding a suffix beginning with a vowel. (Exceptions: w and x are never doubled.)

This rule can be simplified to the V-C-V Formula.

1. Present the following root words and endings on the blackboard, one at a time.

   Have the child write in colored chalk above the appropriate letters in the root words:

   V for vowel
   C for consonant
   V for vowel (above the initial vowel in the ending)

Example:

```
        v  c   v
     r u n---i n g
```

Root Word	Ending
<u>vc</u>	<u>v</u>
run	ing
sin	er
big	est
drop	ing
red	ish
sun	y
mad	est
stun	ing
dip	er
fat	est
pop	er
scot	ish
fib	er
thin	est
flat	est
job	er

2. It is found that when children physically partici-
pate in an activity, they remember the abstract
concept better. The following exercise serves this
purpose.

Use a chart with pockets into which root words, endings and the additional
letters for doubling can be inserted.

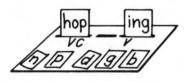

a) The teacher inserts a root word and an
ending.

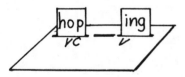

b) She places cards with the appropriate consonants below the chart.

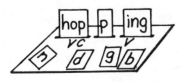

c) The child picks out the consonant that
matches the final letter of the root word and
places it in the pocket.

161

᠉ show comparisons of words that do not double the final consonant in a monosyllabic word when adding a suffix, we use the following exercise.

Short words (one-syllable) can be divided into three groups.

| Group A | | Words ending with a vowel-consonant |
| V C | | Example: <u>rip</u> |

| Group B | | Words ending with a vowel-vowel-consonant |
| V V C | | Example: <u>wood</u> |

Group C		Words ending with a vowel-consonant-
V C C		consonant
		Example: <u>dust</u>

Exercise

Hand out large cards with mixed words to students. Have them sort the words into the appropriate categories under A, B or C.

A	B	C
V C	V V C	V C C
rip	wood	dust
fog	seem	nest

Suggested Words for Sorting Exercise:

spend	lap	dent	fit
hint	shift	tuft	spit
zip	hug	sleep	end
dim	blush	romp	grab
brisk	creep	stop	pet
spin	feel	grip	feed
stain	beg	paint	read
dunk	load	plan	swim
join	top	cool	cram
hop	tan	feel	slip

4. Give a list of suffixes which can be divided into two groups.

Group A
—
V

Suffixes beginning with a vowel

Group B
—
C

Suffixes beginning with a consonant

A — v	B — c
er	ness
ish	ly

Suggested List of Suffixes

est	ing	y	er
ed	ly	ness	en
ish	ful	ment	ence
able	ent	less	

For Older Pupils

These suffixes usually occur in polysyllabic words. <u>Affix and Root Cards,</u> available from Educators Publishing Service (see page 21), contain suffixes and other word parts for useful drill.

hood	some	ant	sion
ancy	ive	ence	ian
ment	ary	ency	ate
ance	ible	tion	ory
ous			

When you combine Group A words	with Group A suffixes,	double the final consonant of Group A words.
V C — r u n +	V — i n g	= ru n n i n g

*Dorothy M. Bywaters, <u>Affix and Root Cards</u>, available from Educators Publishing Service, Inc.

MIXED DRILL

The following exercises should be mimeographed for additional V-C-V drill.

Combine the root words and suffixes using the V-C-V rule.

run + ing	= running
big + er	= _____
sin + ing	= _____
brim + ful	= _____
rust + ed	= _____
spoon + ed	= _____
lilt + ing	= _____
stamp + ed	= _____
war + ing	= _____
dust + y	= _____
trim + est	= _____
sad + ness	= _____
seem + ly	= _____
thin + ness	= _____
man + ly	= _____
paint + ing	= _____
dab + ed	= _____
flat + er	= _____
slush + y	= _____

Choose one of the suffixes from the group listed below. Add it to the phrase, being careful to use the V-C-V rule when appropriate.

ed – y – ing – est – er – ly – en – less – ish – ful

stamp	_____	about
wish	_____	thinking
lilt	_____	songs
rust	_____	fence
stamp	_____	envelope
flat	_____	out
slush	_____	snow
dim	_____	lights
twist	_____	rope
damp	_____	towels
list	_____	baby
chill	_____	morning
gust	_____	wind
fret	_____	baby
red	_____	hair
fur	_____	seal

The following can be given on mimeographed sheets as a spelling exercise using the V-C-V rule.

Fill in the blanks with the correct spelling

Jack slip____ while run ____ to get the shop ____cart.
We are think____ of travel ____over the dust____ roads.
It is not man____ to go beg ____ for tips.
Nancy drop ____the dish when the dog jump ____ .
The car rust ____when it was chip ____ .
Plan ____ is better than wish____think ____ .
Ann glad ____ ship ____ the wed ____gift to Jane.
It is fool____to go swim ____when it is storm____ .
He trim ____ and weed ____the pot____plant before ship ____ it to the shop.
The rob ____grab ____the can ____plums from the shop____ cart.

SUFFIX: <u>ed</u>

When something happened some time ago, whether it was a long time ago or "a moment ago," you add <u>ed</u> to the verb regardless of whether it sounds like (ĕd), (d) or (t).

An easy way to teach the difference between simple nouns and verbs is: "If you can touch it, it is a noun: if you can do it, it is a verb."

(ĕd) Sound

Present Tense	Past Tense – Pronounced (ĕd)
land	landed
melt	melted
grant	granted
last	lasted
hunt	hunted
act	acted
sift	sifted
crust	crusted
nest	nested
pad	padded
feast	feasted
plot	plotted
need	needed

(d) Sound

Present Tense	Past Tense – Pronounced (d)
play	played
trim	trimmed
smell	smelled
stop	stopped
spell	spelled
yell	yelled
grin	grinned
mill	milled
grab	grabbed
rob	robbed
room	roomed
scrub	scrubbed

(continued)

burn	burned
sun	sunned
bloom	bloomed
fill	filled
mull	mulled
sail	sailed
spray	sprayed

(t) Sound

Present Tense	Past Tense — Pronounced (t)
rush	rushed
slip	slipped
dish	dished
crush	crushed
rock	rocked
hump	humped
check	checked
pinch	pinched
bump	bumped
swish	swished
hush	hushed
park	parked
yank	yanked
spank	spanked
wink	winked
stamp	stamped
trick	tricked
ask	asked

Story for Dictation and/or Reading

Ouch!

I went to the beach over the weekend. The sun was bright and broiling. It burned my skin a reddish shade. It hurt! I needed help. Mom sprayed me with sunburn oil. That stopped the hurting. Then I felt much better.

—contributed by Carolyn Smith

 **ew** (as in gr<u>ew</u>)

The teacher reaches with both arms to the ceiling and has the children do the same.

Words for Spelling and Reading

yew*	brew	drew	strew
crew	chew	slew	threw
blew	flew	screw	

Sentences for Dictation and Reading

The notes <u>were</u> strewn by the wind.
Can you unscrew the lock and fix it?
Do not chew the gum that Sam threw out.
<u>Who</u> drew that large mule on the wall?
An ice cream <u>soda</u> is a tasty brew.

*yew — a tree or bush with evergreen leaves

 (as in <u>eigh</u>t)

This is the first four-letter sound we learn.

Words for Spelling and Reading

eight	weigh	neigh	freight
sleigh	weight	inveigh*	

Sentences for Dictation and Reading

It is fun to ride on a sleigh.
Tell him to weigh the freight.
She weighs sixty-eight pounds.
Can you tell the weight of the pig?

Words for Reading Only

eighteen   eighty   eighty-eight   neighbor

Sentences for Reading Only

Her neighbor has eight sleighs.
<u>Grandmother</u> had her eighty-eighth birthday.
The baby weighs eighteen pounds.

*inveigh — to attack with bitter words

ie (as in chief)

Rule: "i before e except after c "
Mnemonic: The i comes first.
                "I am the thief of Bagdad."

Words for Spelling and Reading

chief	bier	field	priest
thief	grief	wield	belief
tier	brief	yield	relief
pier	shriek	shield	

Sentences for Dictation and Reading

The chief will nab the thief.
He left his shield in the field.
It is a relief to get a brief test.
The priest will help him in his grief.
Eight players waited on the baseball field.

Words for Reading Only

niece	piece	siege	pierce
fierce	grieves	thieves	cashier
frontier	fiercely	believe	achieve
shielded			

    A few exceptions to the rule above are:

seize	either	neither	leisure

Sentences for Reading Only

Neither Tom nor Sam had time for leisure.
Do you believe his niece left with the thieves?
I believe the cashier gave you too much change.
The men shielded the children in the battle at the frontier.
They can either seize the time or plan things better.

 **eu** (as in <u>Eu</u>rope or <u>neu</u>tral)

Words for Reading Only

neuter	neutral	euphony	neural
Teuton	feudal	neuron	feud
neuritis	Europe		

Sentences for Reading Only

At times a feudal lord will help his serf.
James was neutral in the feud between the men.

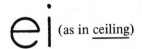 (as in <u>ceiling</u>)

Rule: "<u>i</u> before <u>e</u> except after <u>c</u> "

Words for Reading Only

ceiling
deceit

receive
receipt

deceive

Sentences for Reading Only

The ceiling will receive a coat of paint.
Magic can deceive a <u>person</u>.

tion (as in action)

The pattern tion is used at the end of a word and is the most frequent spelling of the (shun) sound. It is the spelling to use in making nouns from verbs ending in t or te, as educate — education, act — action.

1. Cut off the ending with a red pencil or with the "rule of thumb."
2. Read the word.

Develop this exercise gradually according to the sequence taught.

Words for Spelling and Reading

The following words have a short vowel followed by a consonant before the tion ending.

action	mention	friction	junction
traction	fraction	diction	question
suction	section	dictionary	

In the following words, tion comes after a long vowel and, thus, the vowel says its name before the ending.

notion	nation	lotion	plantation
motion	ration	vacation	education
station	invitation		

Sentences for Dictation and Reading

A tire must have traction.
A big section of the station fell.
Do you have any question on fractions?
Did you mention that we must take action?

Words for Reading Only

auction	portion	objection
caution	direction	correction
affection	digestion	recitation
affliction	position	attention
connection	addition	decoration
solution	collection	foundation

Sentences for Reading Only

You <u>should</u> approach a <u>busy</u> road with caution.
You must pay attention when you attend an auction.
Do you have an objection to a collection of decorations?
<u>Some</u> farms in the South <u>are</u> called plantations.

 (as in <u>rescue</u>)

Words for Spelling and Reading

hue	sue	subdue	continue
due	rescue	argue	retinue
cue	revenue	avenue	

Sentences for Dictation and Reading

I hope you can continue to subdue the men.
The state must get the revenue that is due to it.
Do not argue while driving on the avenue.
Will you continue the rescue <u>work</u>?

Words for Reading Only

tissue	virtue	pursue
statue	issue	curlicue

Sentences for Reading Only

It will be a virtue to pursue the men <u>who</u> stole the statue.
Tell them not to make a hole in the tissue.
The statue is due for a <u>good</u> cleaning.

sion  (as in <u>division</u>)

Words for Spelling and Reading

division	infusion	transfusion
confusion	intrusion	explosion
invasion	inclusion	television

Sentences for Dictation and Reading

An invasion can cause confusion.
I must try to do the problem in division.
I like to see my sister act in a play on television.

Words for Reading Only

excursion	conclusion	decision
collision	provision	vision
seclusion		

Sentences for Reading Only

Do you have <u>good</u> vision?
The excursion will be at the conclusion of the trip.
A decision must be made <u>about</u> provisions for the trip.

ALTERNATE PRONUNCIATIONS

Some of the vowel digraphs in our language have more than one pronunciation. We tell the child that, when he is trying to decode a word, he should try the first sound he has learned and, if it does not make sense, he should then use the second choice.

We follow this with second choices for digraphs and diphthongs taught.

	First Choice		Second Choice		Third Choice	
OW	clown	p. 119	snow	p. 178		
EA	eat	p. 98	head	p. 180	great	p. 188
OO	zoo	p. 130	good	p.181		
EW	grew	p. 168	few	p. 182		
EI	ceiling	p. 172	vein	p. 183		
UE	rescue	p. 175	true	p. 184		
OU	ouch	p. 121	group	p. 185		
SION	division	p. 176	mansion	p. 186		

Consonant Sounds

	First Choice		Second Choice		Third Choice	
S	sit	p. 51	is	p. 66, 190		
CH	chin	p. 42	school	p. 179	machine	p. 189

OW  (as in <u>snow</u>)

This is usually at the end of a word. In other locations, this is the second-choice pronunciation for the letters <u>ow</u>.

Words for Spelling and Reading

low	grow	mown	window
mow	glow	sown	elbow
own	crow	blown	widow
bow	snow	grown	shadow
row	throw	flown	lowly
show	stow	thrown	slowly
blow	bowl	growth	crowbar
flow			

Sentences for Dictation and Reading

I like to see the snow blow.
The bowl made a shadow on the desk.
The pods <u>were</u> slowly blown by the wind.
Did you throw the bowl out of the window?
If you throw grass seed on the snow, will it grow?
I hope I can make <u>good</u> decisions <u>about</u> shows to <u>watch</u>.

Words for Reading Only

yellow	hollow	mellow	pillow
willow	follow	fellow	sparrow
fallow			

Sentences for Reading Only

The yellow willow will bud in the spring.
The sparrow will follow the birds south.
It is nice of that fellow to lend me his pillow.

 **ch** (as in <u>school</u>)

This is the second-choice pronunciation of the digraph <u>ch</u>.

Words for Spelling and Reading

school	Christmas	ache
stomach	echo	chorus

Sentences for Dictation and Reading

The echo shook the window. It gave me a headache.
<u>What</u> <u>does</u> the school bell mean when it rings in the morning?
A puppy has a fat stomach.
Do you sing in the school chorus?
Do you like to see decorations at Christmas?

Words for Reading Only

bronchitis   technical

 ea (as in head)

Point to the head as a signal. This is the second-choice pronunciation of the vowel digraph ea.

Words for Spelling and Reading

read	bread	meant	ready
dead	tread	realm	steady
lead	health	breast	instead
deaf	wealth	heavy	treadle
death	thread	spread	

Sentences for Dictation and Reading

Jan meant to get the heavy thread.
I like to spread my bread with jam.
Are you ready to make the treadle steady?
He meant to be ready to avoid confusion.

Words for Reading Only

feather	meadow	pleasant*	heaven
leather	sweater	dreadful	breakfast
weather	weapon	pheasant*	

Sentences for Reading Only

It is fun to run in the meadow in fine weather.
I think I will trim the sweater with leather.
It is not pleasant to be tickled with a feather.*

*See s as (z) in the middle of words, page 190.

 **OO** (as in good)

This is the second-choice pronunciation for oo in the middle of a word.

Words for Spelling and Reading

cook	look	woof	woodshed
good	foot	stood	cooking
hood	wool	brook	fishhook
took	shook	crook	hoodwink
hook	wood	rooky	hooking

Sentences for Dictation and Reading

Glen shook the wool to fluff it up.
Nan took the wood to the woodshed.
We have a good cook to do the cooking.
He stood by the brook to catch a fish on his hook.

Words for Reading Only

cooker   woolen   understood   undertook

Sentences for Reading Only

Polly undertook the task of cleaning the cooker.
She understood that the woolen dress might shrink.

ew  (as in few)

This is the second-choice pronunciation for ew. A number of words, such as stew, are pronounced either way.

"Just a few words use this sound."

Words for Spelling and Reading

mew	few	stew	renew
new	hew	skew	sinew
dew			

Sentences for Dictation and Reading

Can you hew a few logs?
The new dew smells fresh.
The few new cats did mew when they sat in the dew.
I shall cook a stew in my new pot.
Will you renew your subscription?

Words for Reading Only

pewter	curfew	ewe
mildew	nephew	

Sentences for Reading Only

His nephew will renew the book.
We were glad to see the new nephew.
Jack will stew when he hears of the curfew.
Tell your nephew that pewter will not mildew.
A pewter pitcher is pretty to look at.

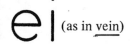 (as in <u>vein</u>)

This is second-choice pronunciation of <u>ei</u>.
Tell the children to look at the <u>veins</u> on their wrists.

skein   rein   veil
reindeer

Sentences for Reading Only

The veil cast a shadow on her face.
Reindeer are supposed to <u>pull</u> Santa's sleigh.

 (as in <u>true</u>)

This is the second-choice pronunciation of <u>ue</u>.

rue	true	flue	misconstrue
glue	blue	construe	

Sentences for Dictation and Reading

(Pupils should write out their own answers to the questions.)

Is it true that the stream is blue?
He lit a fire in the fireplace, but he forgot to open the flue. <u>What</u> do you think happened?
Airplane glue can make <u>your</u> fingers stick to each other just as well as it can make the wings stick on a plane. Has this ever happened to you?
Do you know <u>what</u> "construe" means? Look it up in the dictionary if you do not.

 **OU** (as in <u>group</u>)

This is the second-choice pronunciation of <u>ou</u>.

croup	soup	youth
group	route	. you
you	troupe	

Sentences for Dictation and Reading

Can you make hot soup for the group?
In my youth I <u>often</u> got the croup.
Did you ever belong to an acting troupe?
Turkey soup is a treat to eat.

Exceptions

There is a silent e at the end of <u>route</u> and <u>troupe</u>.
The circus troup<u>e</u> <u>could</u> not find Rout<u>e</u> E.

185

sion  (as in <u>mansion</u>)

This is the second-choice pronunciation of the ending <u>sion</u>.

Words for Spelling and Reading

pension	compulsion	suspension
tension	pretension	expansion
mansion	propulsion	extension

Sentences for Dictation and Reading

Bob and Bill will plan for the expansion.
I have a compulsion to get a big mansion.
<u>Mr</u>. Jones got an extension on his pension.

Words for Reading Only

fission	session	suppression
omission	expression	confession
permission	oppression	compression
mission	transgression	submission

Sentences for Reading Only

We need permission to leave for our mission.
His confession was an admission of a transgression.
A sad expression was on the puppy's face.

Review Sentences for Reading or Spelling — <u>tion</u>

Did you get an invitation to the party?
We went fishing during our vacation.
Our nation is called the United States of <u>America</u>.
If you have a question <u>about</u> the spelling of a word, you should look it up in the dictionary.
I have a collection of stamps and coins.
In June I hope to get a promotion to the next grade.
<u>What</u> relation is your sister to your <u>mother</u>?

Mixed Sentences — <u>tion, sion</u>

My decision is to take a long vacation.
Division is part of education.
<u>There</u> is a lot of confusion at the railroad station.
The explosion was at the old plantation.

 **ea** (as in <u>great</u>)

This is a third choice for <u>ea</u>.

Isn't it GREAT, you have learned all of your sounds?

Ready for a BREAK with a GREAT big STEAK?

Sentences for Dictation and Spelling

Do you think it is great to cook steak on a grill?
I <u>watched</u> the waves break over the rocks.
Did the window break when he threw the ball at it?

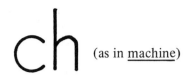 **ch** (as in <u>machine</u>)

This unusual sound for <u>ch</u> appears in words derived from French. Young pupils should learn it for reading only.

cache*	machine	brochure
chute	Chicago	parachute

Sentences for Reading or Dictation

The snow machine <u>would</u> not pick up the sleet.
Have you ever used a laundry chute?
<u>Would</u> you like to jump from a plane in a parachute?
Chicago is <u>sometimes</u> called "The Windy City."
Do you think "to cache" and "to hide away" mean the same thing?

*cache — a place for hiding valuables or provisions; to put something in a cache

S (as in i_s_)

This is the second-choice pronunciation for single _s_ anywhere except at the beginning of a word.

Words for Reading and Spelling

easel	music	clumsy	result
miser	pansy	poison	resort
chosen	rosary	wisdom	present
pleasant	deposit		

No spelling generalization can help pupils determine when to spell (z) with the letter _s_. Tell them that the _s_ spelling is more common than _z_ for the (z) sound _within_ or _at the end of_ a word, but that when in doubt, they should consult a dictionary.

Sentences for Dictation and Reading

It is wise to deposit _your_ funds in a bank.
A music stand is rather like an easel.
It is a pleasant surprise to get a present.
Touching poison ivy can result in a rash.

AFFIXES AND ROOT WORDS:
AN APPROACH FOR THE ADVANCED STUDENT

Building Blocks for an Expanding Vocabulary

Learning to recognize prefixes and suffixes enables us to cut off the stable, familiar parts of a word in order to shorten it and make it easier to spell and read.

Knowing the meanings of prefixes, suffixes and root words helps us to define the word.* To help the student remember the meanings which are given for the affixes and root words we try to associate them with familiar words. The following material is presented as a "chain reaction" to give the creative teacher and her students a model for associating affixes, root words and their meanings.

1.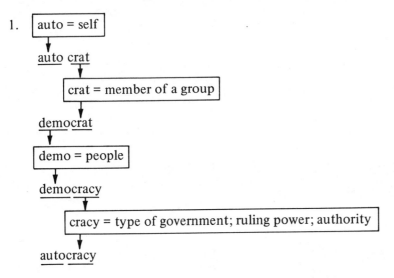

*Affix and Root Cards available from the publisher are useful in teaching these elements.

2.

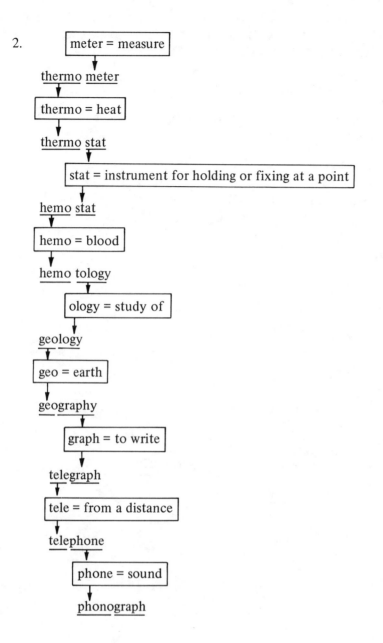

meter = measure

thermo meter

thermo = heat

thermo stat

stat = instrument for holding or fixing at a point

hemo stat

hemo = blood

hemo tology

ology = study of

geology

geo = earth

geography

graph = to write

telegraph

tele = from a distance

telephone

phone = sound

phonograph

3.

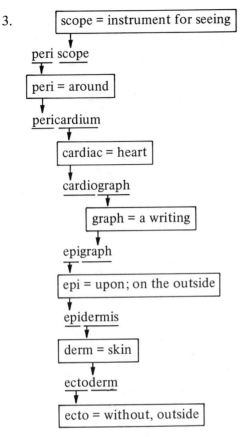

scope = instrument for seeing

peri scope

peri = around

pericardium

cardiac = heart

cardiograph

graph = a writing

epigraph

epi = upon; on the outside

epidermis

derm = skin

ectoderm

ecto = without, outside

The lists of affixes and root words that follow can be incorporated into "chains" similar to the models presented above. This type of associative thinking promotes better retention of the material learned.

PREFIXES

Prefix	Meaning	Example
a, ab	from, without, away	avert, absent
ac, ad, af, al	to, toward	acclimate, advance, affix, allure
alti	high, height	altitude
ambi	both, about	ambidextrous, ambivalent
amphi	around	amphitheatre
ante	before, in front of	antedate
anti	against, opposed	antisocial
auto	of oneself, self	automatic, automobile
be	thoroughly, make	bespatter, belittle
bi	two, double	bicycle, bicuspid
biblio	book	bibliography
bon	good	bonfire, bon voyage
centre	center	centralize
circum	around	circumference
co	with	cooperate, cohesive
col, com, con, cor	together, with	colleague, complete, concurrent, correspond
contra, counter	against	contradict, counteract
de	down from	decrease, descend
demi	half	demigod
dia	through, across	diameter
dif, dis	apart from, from	diffuse, disjoint
dis	not, opposite of	dislike
duo	two	duodecimal
dyna	power	dynamo, dynamic
dys	ill, difficult	dyspeptic
e, ex	out, from, away	egress, exit, export
em, en, ento	in, into	embroil, engross
epi	upon, on the outside	epidermis
eu	well, good	eulogy
extra	beyond	extraordinary
for	away, not	forbid
fore	in front of	forecast, foretell
hemi	half	hemisphere
hetero	different	heterogeneous
holo	whole, all	holocaust
hyper	above, too much	hypersensitive

Prefix	Meaning	Example
idio	one's own	idiom
il, im, ir	not	illegal, impossible, irresponsible
in	in, into, not	inside, inaccurate
inter	between	interstate
intra	within	intramural
iso	equal, same	isometric, isocracy
kilo	one thousand	kilocycle
macro	large, long	macrocosm, macroscopic
magni	great	magnify
mal	bad, wrong	malpractice
micro	small	microphone, microscopic
mis	wrongly	misquote
mono	single, alone	monoplane, monologue
multi	many	multiply, multitude
non	not	nonsense
nov	nine	November
octo	eight	octopus, octave
oligo	few	oligarchy
orni	bird	ornithology
ortho	straight, right	orthodox
pan	whole	panorama, Pan-American
pedi	foot	pedicure
penta	five	pentagon
per	through	perceive
peri	around, round	perimeter, periphery
phono	voice, tone	phonograph
poly	many	polygamy
post	after	postscript
pre	before	predate, prefix
pro	forward	progress, proceed
pseudo	false	pseudonym, pseudoclassic
quadri	four	quadruped, quadruplicate
quint	five	quintuplet, quintet
re	back, again	regain, recount
retro	backward	retrospect, retroactive
se	aside, apart	separate
semi	half	semicircle
sext	six	sextet
sub, sup, sus	under, below	subway, support, sustain

Prefix	Meaning	Example
super	above	superimpose, superintendent
syl, sym, syn	with, together	syllable, sympathy, synchronize
tele	far	telephone
tetra	four	tetrameter
theo	God	theology
to	this, the	today
trans	across	transfer, transcontinental
tri	three	tripod, triangle
ultra	excessive	ultraconservative
un	not, opposite	unhappy, unwilling
uni	one	united
vice	in place of	vice-president
with	back, away	withheld

SUFFIXES

Suffix	Meaning	Example
able	possible to	likable, manageable
acity	quality of	audacity
acious	given to	audacious
acy	state of being	privacy
age	act of, state of, place	homage, hermitage
al	referring to, like	natural, homicidal
an	of, having to do with	American, African
ance	act, fact of	guidance
ancy	act of	constancy
ant	being, one who	assistant
ar	like, one who	liar, circular
arium	place for	aquarium, planetarium
ary	having to do with	revolutionary, stationary
ate	one who, to make	mandate, dictate
ation	of, state of	admiration, explanation
active	tending to	talkative

Suffix	Meaning	Example
cle	little	particle
cracy	type of government-authority	democracy
cule	little	miniscule
dom	state, authority of	kingdom, freedom
ed	action completed, did	consented
en	made of	golden
ence, ency	state of, act of	confidence, emergency
ent, er	one who, that which	correspondent, teacher, rocker
er (adj.)	more than	greater
est	most	smartest
esque	like in manner or style	grotesque, picturesque
ful	full of	helpful, deceitful
fy	to make, to form	magnify, dignify
hood	state of	brotherhood
ial	on account of	official
ian	one who	physician
ible	capable of being, able	horrible
ic	like, having to do with	historic
icity	quality of	domesticity, electricity
ify	to make, to form	falsify, clarify
ile	capable of, suited to	infantile, senile
ing	action going on, result of action	acting, living
ion	act of doing	confession
ish	resembling, like	boyish, stylish
ism	quality or doctrine of	capitalism, socialism
ist	one who	scientist
itis	inflammation of	bronchitis
ity	quality or state of	creativity
ive	inclined to, that which	detective, reflective
ize	to make, practice	theorize, eulogize
kin	little	lambkin
less	without	witless, harmless
let	small, little	droplet, starlet
like	resembling	homelike
ly	manner of acting, like	quickly, quietly

Suffix	Meaning	Example
ment	state of, act of	employment, enjoyment
meter	instrument of measuring	speedometer
ness	state or quality of being	sharpness
or	one who, that which	sailor
ory	serving for, place where	conservatory
ose	abounding in, full of	verbose
osis	illness of	psychosis
osity	state or quality of being	generosity
ous	full of	dangerous
ship	quality or condition	friendship
sion, tion	state of, act of	cooperation, pretension
some	more, the same as	quarrelsome
tude	quality or degree of	certitude
ty	state of, act of	certainty
ure	one who, result of	failure
ward	in direction of, toward	homeward
y	marked by	healthy, wealthy

ROOT WORDS

Root Word	Meaning	Example
acri	sharp, bitter	acrid, acrimony
acro	highest point	acropolis, acrobat
act	rouse, doing	acting, activate
aesth	perceiving	aesthetic
ag	do, act	agenda, agitate
ami	friend	amicable
ann	year	anniversary
anthrop	man	anthropology
api	bee	apiary
aqua	water	aquaduct
aster, astr	star	asterisk, astronomy
audi, audio	hear	auditorium, audiovisual
avi	bird	aviary
bar	weight, pressure	barometer
bene	well, good	beneficial, benefactor

Root Word	Meaning	Example
bio	life	biology
cant	sing	cantata
cap	to take	capacity
capit	head	capital
carcer	prison	incarcerate
cardia	heart	cardiac
ceed, cede, cess	go, move, yield	recede, proceed, access
ceive	take	conceive
celer	quick	accelerate
cent	hundred	percent, centimeter, century
chron	time	chronicle, chronic
cide	kill	homicide
corp	body	corporate, corpulent
cosm	universe	cosmic, cosmology
crat	member of a group	autocrat, aristocrat
cred	belief	credible, credit
crypt	hidden, secret	cryptic
cur	flow	current
dec, deci	ten	decimal, decade
demo	people	democrat, demography
dent	tooth	dentist, dentifrice
derm	skin	dermatology, epidermis
dextr	right hand	dextrous, dextral
dic, dict	say, speak	dictate, dictaphone
divid, divis	separate	divident, divisible
doc	to teach	indoctrinate, doctrine
dont	teeth	orthodontic
dome	house	domestic, domicile
domin	rule, master	dominate
don	give	donate
duc, duct	to lead	conduct, conductor
dulc	sweet	dulcet
dupl	to double	duplicate
dur	to last	duration
ego	I, self	egotist, egomaniac
entom	insect	entomology
equ	horse	equine
equa	equal	equality
eros	love	erotic
err	to go astray, to do wrong	errant, erratic

Root Word	Meaning	Example
fall	to mistake, deceive	fallacy
fel	cat	feline
fer	carry	transfer, refer
fin	end	final, finish
flagr	burn	conflagration
fid	faith	confident
fort	make strong	comfort, fortify
frater	brother	fraternity
gam	marriage	bigamy, monogamy
garrul	chatter	garrulous
gene	race, sex	genetic, geneology
geo	earth	geography, geology
gloss, glot	language, tongue	glossary
grad	step	gradually
graph	a writing instrument for making records	epigraph, graphic
grat	thank	gratitude, grateful
hydr	water	hydraulic, dehydrate
ichth	fish	ichthyology
icon	image, idol	iconoclast
ign	fire	ignite
ject	throw	inject, project
junct	join	junction, injunction
lat	carry, bear	relate
laud	praise	applaud, laudable
lect	to choose	select, elect
leg	law	legal
lith	stone	monolith
loc	place	locate
locu, logue, loqu	to speak	elocution, monologue, eloquent
logy	to study	geology, zoology
luc	to be light, clear	lucid, lucent
lun	moon	lunar
man, manu	hand	manicure, manifest manuscript
maxim	largest	maximum
medi	middle	mediocre
memo	to remember	memorable, commemorate
ment	act, way	judgement, statement
meter, metr	to measure	metrology, metric
mim	imitate	mimic

Root Word	Meaning	Example
min	smallest	minimize
mis, mit	to send	mission, remit
morph	form, one characterized by	morphic, amorphous
mort	death	mortal
nasc, nat	to be born	nascent, native
neo	new	neophyte
nephr	kidney	nephritis
neur	nerve	neurosis neurology
neutr	neither	neutral
nomen	name	nomenclature
nov	new	novice nova
omni	all	omnipotent
ophthal	eye	ophthalmic
osteo	bone	osteopath
ov	egg	ovum
pac	peace	pacify
pater, patri	father	paternal, patrimony
pedia	child	pediatrician
ped	foot	pedicure, biped
patho	suffering	pathological, pathos
pel	drives	compel
pend	hang	pendulum
penetr	go through	penetrate
petr	rock	petrify
photo, phos	light	photography, phosphorus
phob	fear	hydrophobia
pod	foot	podiatrist, tripod
port	carry	transport, portable
pos	to place	deposit
pot	power	despot, potent
puls	drive, force	compulsive
pyro	fire	pyromaniac
ques, quiro	to ask	request, question
quie	rest	quietly
radi	ray	radiant, radiator
rect	right, straight	erect, correct
regu	rule, model	regulate, irregular
rhino	nose	rhinitis

Root Word	Meaning	Example
rupt	to break	disrupt
sacr, sanct	holy, sacred	sacramental, sanctify
sal	salt	saline, salty
salut	health	salutary
salve	safe	salvation, salvage
sangui	blood	sanguine
sani	healthy, sound	sanitary, sanity
sarco	flesh	sarcoma
sati	gratify	satisfy, satisfaction
scend	to climb	ascend, descend
schizo	to split	schizophrenic
schol	school	scholastic
scien	knowledge, skill	scientific
scler, sclero	hard	sclerosis
scope	see, observe	microscope
scrib, script	to write	scribble, inscription
sect	to cut, divide	bisect, vivisection
seism	earthquake	seismogram
sens, senti	feel, think, perceive	sensation, sentiment
sequ	to follow	sequel
sign	a symbol, mark	signify, signature
simil, simul	same, same time	similar, simultaneous
spec, spect	look, behold	speculate, spectator
speci	particular sort, kind	specimen, species
spher	ball, globular	sphere, spherical
spir	breath	respiration
sta	stand	station, stationary
tend, tens	stretch	distend, tension
therm	heat	thermometer
tort	twist	distort
tract	draw	distract, detract
utili	useful	utility, utilize
vent	come, arrive	convene, convention
veri	truth	verify, veritable
vert, ver	turn	revert, invert
vid, vis	to see	video, visible
viv	to live	vivid, vivacious
voc	voice	vocalize
vor, vore	to eat	voracious, carnivore
zo	animal	zoology, zoography

SPELLING WITH AFFIXES

Words ending in "magic (silent) _e_" usually ➤	drop the _e_ before a suffix beginning with a vowel and ➤	keep the _e_ before a suffix beginning with a consonant.
use	using	useful
hope	hoping	hopeful
love	lovable	lovely
close	closest	closely
sincere	sincerest	sincerely
late	later	lateness
care	cared	careless
drive	driving	driveway
like	liked	likeness
name	naming	namely
fine	finer	finely
shame	ashamed	shameful
mere	merest	merely
safe	safer	safely

"When _I_ comes in, '_e_ goes out."

When a verb ends in silent e, ➤	we usually drop the _e_ before adding _ing_ ➤	but not when adding other suffixes.
state	stating	statement
excite	exciting	excitement
improve	improving	improvement
tune	tuning	tuneful
hate	hating	hateful
move	moving	movement
complete	completing	completeness

203

Words ending in ce and ge		keep the e when adding suffixes beginning with a, o or u, in order to retain the soft c and g sounds.
notice	noticing	noticeable
manage	managing	manageable
service	servicing	serviceable
pronounce	pronouncing	pronounceable
trace	tracing	traceable
change	changing	changeable
charge	charging	chargeable
outrage	outraged	outrageous
advantage	advantaged	advantageous
replace	replacing	replaceable

The following exceptions can be readily memorized through the use of the following sentence:

"There is little ARGUMENT and complete ACKNOWLEDGMENT that if the day of JUDGMENT will DULY, TRULY come, it will be WHOLLY AWFUL."

****

The e is kept in the following words in order to preserve their identity and to keep their pronunciation intact.

acreage	canoeing	dyeing
hoeing	mileage	shoeing
singeing	tingeing	toeing

****

Words ending in a y preceded by a consonant ⟶	usually change the y to an i before all suffixes ⟶	except those beginning with an i.
cry	cried	crying
signify	signified	signifying
study	studies	studying
try	tries	trying
imply	implies	implying
reply	replies	replying
identify	identifies	identifying
envy	envies	envying
baby	babies	babyish
ferry	ferried	ferrying
glorify	glorified	glorifying
horrify	horrified	horrifying
copy	copied	copyist
deny	denied	denying
hurry	hurried	hurrying
supply	supplied	supplying
bury	buried	burying
lobby	lobbied	lobbyist

Words ending in a y preceded by a vowel ⟶	retain the y when adding a suffix.	
enjoy	enjoying	enjoyable
play	playing	played
delay	delaying	delayed
employ	employing	employable
pray	praying	prayed

WHICH TO USE?

Suffix: <u>sede</u> — <u>ceed</u> — <u>cede</u>
(to withdraw, yield, grant, assign)

Which to use?

<u>sede</u>: Only one word ends in <u>sede</u>.
SUPERSEDE

<u>ceed</u>: Only three to remember for <u>ceed</u>.
"You will SUCCEED if you PROCEED to
EXCEED your sales."

<u>cede</u>: All the rest are spelled <u>cede</u>.
precede, accede, recede-------------

****

Endings: <u>cle</u> and <u>cal</u> sound alike

Which to use?

<u>cle</u>: This one is always a noun ending.
bicycle	icicle	uncle
vehicle	cuticle	

<u>cal</u>: This one is an adjective ending.
physical	tropical	vertical

Endings: <u>us</u> and <u>ous</u> sound alike.

Which to use?

<u>us</u>: This one is always a noun ending.
focus	octopus

<u>ous</u>: This one is always an adjective ending.
famous	perilous

****

APPENDIX

INDEX TO PHONETIC READERS

According to Position in Recipe for Reading Sequence
Compiled by Barbara K. Lynds and Carolyn Smith

The index which follows corresponds to the recommended teaching sequence of this manual. Phonetic elements appear in the left column according to the order in which they are taught. Appropriate books for reading at each stage in the sequence are listed at the right.

The list is cumulative. Thus the book Hap and Pam (letter p) should not be introduced until the preceding letters – c, o, a, d, g, m, l, h, t, i, j, and k – have also been mastered. Books listed as supplementary readers may require additional letters as noted in the comments.

A storybook located at a given point in the sequence may also be used by the student at any later time.

Position in Recipe for Reading Sequence	Phonetic Reader
c o a d g m l h t	*Cat and Cod* (Ed. Pub. – Recipe for Reading)
	Supplementary readers for $\breve{a}$ – contain most consonants.
	Merrill Linguistic Readers, level 1 (Merrill) Let's Read Series 1 (Barnhart)
i	*A Hog is Ham?!* (Ed. Pub. – Recipe for Reading)
	Supplementary readers for $\breve{i}$ – contain most consonants.
	Biff and Tiff (Heath-Miami) *Kid Kit and the Catfish* (Heath-Miami)
	Supplementary readers for $\breve{a}$ and $\breve{i}$ – contain most consonants.
	A Pig Can Jig (SRA) *Nat the Rat* (Heath-Miami)
j	*Jim and Tim* (Ed. Pub. – Recipe for Reading)
k	*Kim Has a Hat* (Ed. Pub. – Recipe for Reading)

p	*Hap and Pam* (Ed. Pub. — Recipe for Reading)
ch	*Chad* (Ed. Pub. — Recipe for Reading)
u	*Chug-Chug* (Ed. Pub. — Recipe for Reading)
	Supplementary readers for ŭ — contain most consonants.
	***Tug Duck and Buzz Bug* (Heath-Miami)** ***The Sack Hut* (Heath-Miami)** **Merrill Linguistic Readers, level 2 (Merrill)**
b	*Bob and the Big Bag* (Ed. Pub. — Recipe for Reading)
r	*The 3 Chums* (Ed. Pub. — Recipe for Reading)
	"?" (Ed. Pub. — Recipe for Reading)
f n	*A Gag* (Ed. Pub. — Recipe for Reading)
	Nan (Ed. Pub. — Recipe for Reading)
e	*Jed and Jip* (Ed. Pub. — Recipe for Reading)
	A Pun Is Fun (Ed. Pub. — Recipe for Reading)
s	*It Is . . .?* (Ed. Pub. — Recipe for Reading)
	Nat (Ed. Pub. — Teaching Box)
	Sam (Ed. Pub. — Teaching Box)
	As Is (Ed. Pub. — Teaching Box)
	A Man Sat (Ed. Pub. — Teaching Box)
	The Cat (Ed. Pub. — Teaching Box)
	Dan (Ed. Pub. — Teaching Box)
	Sol the Sun (Ed. Pub. — Recipe for Reading)
	The Jet (Ed. Pub. — Primary Phonics)
	The Tin Man (Ed. Pub. — Primary Phonics)
	Al (Ed. Pub. — Primary Phonics)
	Tim (Ed. Pub. — Primary Phonics)
	Ted (Ed. Pub. — Primary Phonics)
	Mac and Tab (Ed. Pub. — Primary Phonics)
sh th(as in *that*)	*Rich Sam* (Ed. Pub. — Recipe for Reading)
w	*Sam and Sal* (Ed. Pub. — Recipe for Reading)
	Meg (Ed. Pub. — Primary Phonics)

	Ben Bug (Ed. Pub. – Primary Phonics)
	The Wig (Ed. Pub. – Primary Phonics)
	Ed (Ed. Pub. – Primary Phonics)
wh y	*Yes, Yes, Yes* (Ed. Pub. – Recipe for Reading)
x	*Fox in a Fix* (Ed. Pub. – Recipe for Reading)
v z	*Easy A – Z* (Ed. Pub. – Recipe for Reading)
th (as in *thin*) qu	*The Quiz* (Ed. Pub. – Recipe for Reading)

Supplementary readers with *a e i o u* and all consonants – predominantly consonant-vowel-consonant words.

First Phonics, Part 1 (Ed. Pub.) – vowels *a, i, o* only
Stories for First Phonics, pp. 1-12 (Ed. Pub.)
Little Stories, Group I cards (Ed. Pub. – Gillingham)
Sullivan Storybooks, level 1 (McGraw)
M .W. Sullivan Stories, level 1 (BRL)
Fun Readers, level 1 (BRL)
Palo Alto Reading Program, levels 1-2-3-4 (Har Brace J.)
Let's Read Series, levels 1-2-3 (Barnhart)
Exploring Lands in the Sea, level 1 (Century)

Two-syllable compound words	*A Hen in a Fox's Den* (SRA)
ff ll ss	*Step Up 3* (Ed. Pub.)
	Merrill Linguistic Readers, level 3 (Merrill)
Consonant blends	*Stories for First Phonics* (Ed. Pub.)
	Little Stories, Group II cards (Ed. Pub. – Gillingham)
	Step Up 4 (Ed. Pub.)
	Sullivan Storybooks, levels 2 & 3 (McGraw)
	Reading Goals, The Red Book (Lippincott)
	M.W. Sullivan Stories, levels 2-3 (BRL)
	Six Ducks in a Pond (SRA)
	Exploring Lands in the Sea, levels 2 - 3 (Century)
	Miami Linguistic Readers, levels 3-4-5-6 (Heath)
	Let's Read Series, level 4 (Barnhart)
	Fun Readers, level 2 (BRL)

Is It So? level C 1, pp. 1-47 (Random)

Palo Alto Reading Program, levels 1-2-3-4 (Har Brace J.)

Two-syllable
consonant blends

The Hotrod (Ed. Pub. – Teaching Box)

The Lost Hat (Ed. Pub. – Teaching Box)

Gus and His Sack (Ed. Pub. – Teaching Box)

The Box (Ed. Pub. – Teaching Box)

ing ang ung ong
ink ank unk onk

A King on a Swing (SRA)

Sullivan Storybooks, levels 3-4-5 (McGraw)

M.W. Sullivan Stories, levels 3-4 (BRL)

The Raft (Ed. Pub. – Teaching Box)

Red's One Man Band (Ed. Pub. – Teaching Box)

The Wombat (Ed. Pub. – Teaching Box)

Fun Readers, levels 3-4 (BRL)

Let's Read Series, level 5 (Barnhart)

Merrill Linguistic Readers, level 4, pp. 16-21 (Merrill)

Is It So? level C 1, pp. 47-80 (Random)

First Phonics, Part 2 (Ed. Pub.) – selections

Magic e

The Joke (Ed. Pub. – Primary Phonics) – no blends

The Cake (Ed. Pub. – Primary Phonics) – no biends

Mac Is Safe (Ed. Pub. – Primary Phonics) – no blends

The Big Game (Ed. Pub. – Primary Phonics) – no blends

Little Stories, Group III cards (Ed. Pub. – Gillingham)

Supplementary readers for use after long vowels have
been introduced – predominantly blends with scattered
vowel digraphs and common suffixes.

The Wee Little Man (Follett)
The Splendid Belt of Mr. Big (Follett)

Big Bug Little Bug (Follett)
Six and Six, level C 2 (Random)
The Animal Hat Shop (Follett)
Sad Mrs. Sam Sack (Follett)
Palo Alto Reading Program, levels 6-7-8 (Har Brace J.)

These readers contain appropriate selections for use from this point on:

Reading Goals, The Blue Book (Lippincott) p. 55
Reading Goals, The Orange Book (Lippincott) p. 49

ea ee oa ai ay

The Fire (Ed. Pub. — Primary Phonics) — no blends

Sail (Ed. Pub. — Primary Phonics) — no blends

The Goat (Ed. Pub. — Primary Phonics) — no blends

The Bee (Ed. Pub. — Primary Phonics) — no blends

The Seal (Ed. Pub. — Primary Phonics) — no blends

Hide and Seek (Ed. Pub. — Primary Phonics) — no blends

The Best Gift (Ed. Pub. — Primary Phonics)

Mittens (Ed. Pub. — Primary Phonics)

The Sea Gull (Ed. Pub. — Primary Phonics)

The Lost Duck (Ed. Pub. — Primary Phonics)

Max and the Fox (Ed. Pub. — Primary Phonics)

Slide (Ed. Pub. — Primary Phonics)

The Plane Trip (Ed. Pub. — Primary Phonics)

Spot (Ed. Pub. — Primary Phonics)

The Prints (Ed. Pub. — Primary Phonics)

The Dream (Ed. Pub. — Primary Phonics)

The Elf in the Singing Tree (Follett)

Let's Read Series, levels 6-7 (Barnhart)

Merrill Linguistic Readers, level 5 (Merrill)

er ir ur

Reading Goals, The Blue Book (Lippincott) pp. 14, 27, 37, 63, plus assorted other selections

M.W. Sullivan Stories, level 5 (BRL)

Sullivan Storybooks, level 6 (McGraw) no long vowels

ow ou igh	*Chang's Shell* (Heath-Miami)
	Jack and the Magic Bean (Heath-Miami)
	Fun Readers, level 5 (BRL)
	Exploring Lands in the Sea, level 4 (Century)
-le	*Reading Goals, The Blue Book* (Lippincott) pp. 43, 56
	Reading Goals, The Orange Book (Lippincott) pp. 1, 10
ar or oo	Sullivan Storybooks, level 8 (McGraw)
	M.W. Sullivan Stories, levels 5, 6 (BRL)
	Fun Readers, level 6 (BRL)
	Reading Goals, The Blue Book (Lippincott) pp.1-4, 9, 19, 33
	Reading Goals, The Orange Book (Lippincott) pp. 15, 26, 27
-y ck tch	*The Teacup Whale* (Ed. Pub. – Gillingham)
	Little Stories, *Much Fun* (Ed. Pub. – Gillingham)
	Little Quack (Follett)
Hard/soft c & g, dge	Little Stories, Group IV cards (Ed. Pub. – Gillingham)
	Miami Linguistic Readers, level 7 (Heath-Miami)
	M.W. Sullivan Stories, levels 7-8 (BRL)
	Hide and Seek, level D (Random)
	Fun Readers, levels 7-8 (BRL)
Digraphs	Supplementary readers that are appropriate for the digraphs *au* through *ea* (as in *great*).
	For young readers:
	The Look Book Series – Nature Activity Readers (Ed. Pub.) Miami Linguistic Readers, levels 9-15 (Heath) M.W. Sullivan Stories, levels 9-15 (BRL) Structural Reading Series, levels E, F, and G (Random) Sullivan Storybooks, levels 9-15 (McGraw) Fun Readers, levels 9-12 (BRL)
	For older readers – these have smaller print and fewer pictures than above series:
	Phonetic Readers, books 1-6 (Ed. Pub.) Martin Mooney Minute Mysteries Series (Ed. Pub.) Merrill Linguistic Readers, upper levels (Merrill)

Let's Read Series, levels 8-9 (Barnhart)
Reading Goals, upper levels (Lippincott)
Pacemaker Classics Series (Fearon)
Pacemaker Storybooks Series, sets 1-4 (Fearon)
Pacemaker True Adventure Series (Fearon)

NAME AND ADDRESS OF PUBLISHER

BRL

Behavioral Research Laboratories
(Fun Readers)
(M.W. Sullivan Stories)
Box 577
Palo Alto, California 94302

Barnhart

Clarence L. Barnhart
(Let's Read Series   Bloomfield Readers)
Box 250
Bronxville, New York 10708

Century

Century Communications
(Exploring Lands in the Sea)
San Francisco, California

Ed. Pub.

Educators Publishing Service, Inc.
75 Moulton Street
Cambridge, Massachusetts 02138

Fearon

Fearon Publishers, Educational Division
(Pacemaker Series)
6 Davis Drive
Belmont, California 94002

Follett

Follett Publishing Company
1010 W. Washington Blvd.
Chicago, Illinois 60607

Har Brace J.

Harcourt Brace Jovanovich, Inc.
(Palo Alto Reading Program)
757 Third Avenue
New York, New York 10017

Heath
                     D.C. Heath & Company
                     (Miami Linguistic Readers)
                     125 Spring Street
                     Lexington, Massachusetts 02173

Lippincott
                     J.B. Lippincott Company
                     (Lippincott Basic Reading Series)
                     East Washington Square
                     Philadelphia, Pennsylvania 19105

McGraw
                     McGraw-Hill Book Company, Webster Division
                     (Sullivan Storybooks)
                     Princeton Road
                     Highstown, New Jersey 08520

Merrill
                     Charles E. Merrill Publishing Company
                     (Merrill Linguistic Readers)
                     1300 Alum Creek Drive
                     Columbus, Ohio 43216

Random
                     Random House, Inc., School Division
                     (Structural Reading Series A -E)
                     201 East 50th Street
                     New York, New York 10022

SRA
                     Science Research Associates
                     (SRA Basic Reading Series)
                     259 East Erie Street
                     Chicago, Illinois 60611

BIBLIOGRAPHY

Chatwin, Nora, *Physical Education for Primary Grades.* Ontario, Canada, J.M. Dent and Sons, 1956.

Childs, Sally B. and Childs, Ralph de S., *Magic Squares.* Cambridge, Massachusetts, Educators Publishing Service, Inc., 1967.

Critchley, MacDonald, *Developmental Dyslexia.* London, Wm. Heinemann Ltd., 1966.

Crosby, R.M.N. and Liston, Robert, *The Waysiders.* New York, Delacorte Press, 1968.

Cruickshank, William M., *The Brain-Injured Child in Home, School and Community.* Syracuse, New York, Syracuse University Press, 1967.

Cruickshank, William M. *et al., A Teaching Method for Brain-Injured and Hyperactive Children.* Syracuse, New York, Syracuse University Press, 1967.

De Hirsch, Katrina, *et al., Predicting Reading Failure: A Preliminary Study.* New York, Harper and Row, 1966. Available from Educators Publishing Service, Inc., 75 Moulton Street, Cambridge, Massachusetts 02138.

Delacato, Carl H., *Diagnosis and Treatment of Speech and Reading Problems.* Springfield, Illinois, Charles C. Thomas Company, 1970.

Gillingham, Anna and Stillman, Bessie W., *Remedial Training for Children with Specific Disability in Reading, Spelling, and Penmanship.* (7th edition) Cambridge, Massachusetts, Educators Publishing Service, Inc., 1960.

Kephart, Newell C., *Learning Disability: An Educational Adventure.* Danville, Illinois, Interstate Printers and Publishers, Inc., 1968.

Kephart, Newell C., *The Slow Learner in the Classroom.* Columbus, Ohio, Charles E. Merrill Books, Inc., 1960.

Orton, Samuel T., *Reading, Writing and Speech Problems in Children: A Presentation of Certain Types of Disorders of the Language Faculty.* New York, W.W. Norton and Company, 1964. Available from Educators Publishing Service, Inc., 75 Moulton St., Cambridge, Massachusetts.

Radler, D.W. and Kephart, Newell C., *Success Through Play.* New York, Harper and Row, 1960.

Reading Disorders in the United States. Report of the Secretary's (HEW) National Advisory Committee on Dyslexia and Related Reading Disorders, August, 1969.

Roswell, Florence G. and Natchez, G., *Reading Disability: Diagnosis and Treatment.* New York, Basic Books, 1970.

Stern, Catherine and Gould, T.S., *Children Discover Reading: An Introduction to Structural Reading.* New York, Random House, 1965.

INDEX

a, as in apple, 28
    as in all, 149, 152
Affixes, 191 - 206
    Affix and Root Cards, 191n.
    spelling rules, 203 - 206
ai, as in mail, 102 - 103
Alphabet, as a code, 13
ar, as in star, 127 - 128
au, as in August, 149, 151
Auditory factors, 10, 15
    comprehension, 22
    memory training, 19
aw, as in straw, 149 - 150
ay, as in play, 106

b, 44 - 45
"Bibliography", 12, 24
Blends, consonant, 73 - 83
Blending, 17 - 18
Books, phonetic, 14, 20, 21 - 22, 207 - 213

c, hard, as in cat, 26, 40
    hard and soft, 136 - 138, 204
    review lists, 138, 143
cal, 206
ce, 204
cede, 206
ceed, 206
ch, as in chin, 42
    as in machine, 189
    as in school, 179
    ch/tch spelling rule, 157
ck, as in black, 134
cle, 206
Compound words, 64
Comprehension skills, 6, 22
Consonant blends, 73 - 83
    detached syllables, 77 - 78
    endings -ng, -nk, 80 - 83
    final blends, 74 - 75
    initial blends, 73 - 74
    "magic e" words, 88
    review, 76
    two-syllable words, 79
Crosby, R.M.N., 2, 3, 13n.

d, 29
dge, 142
Dictation exercises, method,
    non-phonetic words, 36
    sentences, 19, 36
    stories, 22
    words, 16, 71
Digraphs,
    consonant, 42, 52, 53, 55, 60, 61, 93, 134,
        152 - 153, 179, 189
    vowel, 94 - 108, 130, 170 - 172, 175, 180 -
        181, 183-5, 188

Diphthongs, 119-122, 153-155, 177-178
Directionality (left-right orientation), 4, 7, 17
Dolch Sight Cards, 72
Dysgraphia, 4
Dyslexia (HEW report), 1
    see also Specific Learning Disabilities

e, as in egg, 49 - 50
ea, as in eat, 98 - 99, 177
    as in great, 177, 188
    as in head, 177, 180
ed (to show past tense), 166 - 167
ee, as in tree, 104 - 105
ei, as in ceiling, 108, 172, 177
    as in vein, 177, 183
eigh, as in eight, 169
Endings, ble-fle-tle-dle-gle-kle-ple-zle, 124 - 125
    in syllable division, 147
    ing, as an ending, 158 - 159
    ing-ang-ong-ung-ink-ank-unk-onk, 80 - 82
    ly, as a suffix, 133
    ly-vy-by-dy-ty-fy-ny-py-sy, 131-132
    sion, 176, 186
    tion, 173 - 174
er, as in her, 113 - 114
eu, as in Europe, 171
    as in rescue, 175
    as in true, 184
ew, as in few, 177, 182
    as in grew, 168, 177

f, 47
ff-ll-ss, 65

g, hard, as in go, 30
    hard and soft, 139 - 143, 204
    review list, 143
Games,
    for vowel digraphs, 97
    phonetic word, 12, 14, 20
ge, 142
Gillingham, Anna, 3

h, 33
Homonyms, 96, 98, 100, 102, 104, 115, 117

i, as in Indian, 38
ie, as in chief, 170
igh, as in light, 123
ild-old words, 126
ing, ending, 158 - 159
ir, as in bird, 113, 115 - 116

j, 39

k, 40, 135
Kinesthetics, 10, 15 - 16

l, 32
Language written, 6, 10, 13
Learning disabilities, 2 - 5

Lesson plan, 15 - 24
Listening for meaning, 22
Long vowel sounds,
    ild-old, etc., 126
    "magic e", 84 - 92
    syllable division, 145 - 147
ly, as a suffix, 133

m, 31
"Magic e", 84 - 92
    detached syllable, 91
    plus affixes, 203 - 204
    review tests, 89 - 90
    tachistoscope for, 86
    two-syllable words containing, 92
    with long vowels and (k) sound, 135
Magic squares, 97, 99
Materials required, 14
Memory training, 19
Mnemonics, 96
Morse code, 13

n, 48
Nonphonetic words, see sight words

o, as in olive, 27
oa, as in soap, 100 - 101
oe, as in toe, 107
oi, as in oil, 153 - 154
old - ost words, 126
Older children, 12 - 13, 133, 191ff.
oo, as in good, 177, 181
    as in zoo, 130, 177
or, as in horn, 129
Orton, Samuel T., 3
ou, as in group, 177, 185
    as in ouch, 119, 121 - 122, 177
ous, 206
ow, as in clown, 119 - 120, 177
    as in snow, 177 - 178
oy, as in boy, 153, 155

p, 41
ph, as in phone, 93
Phonograms, 13
Polysyllabic words, 67 - 68, 70 - 71, 79
    syllable division, 109 - 111, 124 - 125,
                131 - 132, 145 - 148
Prefixes, 191 - 196
Pronunciation rules,
    ge - dge, 142
    hard-soft c, 137
    hard-soft g, 140
    y, as a vowel, 144
Pronunciations, alternate, 177

qu, as in queen, 61

r, 46
Readers, phonetic, 20, 21 - 22, 207ff.
Reading, at home, 23
    comprehension, 22
    documenting progress of, 12
    independent, 21
    oral, 20
Review, 62
Review lists, exercises,
    consonant blends, 76, 78
    consonant-vowel-consonant, 63, 69
    endings, 147
    hard-soft c and g, 143
    "magic e", 89 - 90
    suffixes, adding (VCV rule), 164 - 165
    tion, 187
    two-syllable words, 112, 148
Root words, 161 - 164, 191 - 193, 198 - 202
Routine, daily, 7, 12, 15 - 24
    summary of, 24

s, as in sit, 51
    as in his, 66, 88n., 190
ss, 65
sede, 206
Sentences, dictation of, 19, 36
    reading of, 19 - 20
Sentence cards, 14, 19
Sequence charts, 6
sh, 52
Sight words, 19, 36, 72
Silent e, see "Magic e"
sion, as in division, 176 - 177
    as in mansion, 177, 186 - 187
Sounds, 10, 14ff.
    introducing new, 11 - 12, 37, 73
Specific learning disabilities, 2, 3 - 5
Spelling, 16 - 17
Spelling rules, affixes, 203 - 206
    alternate spellings, 113 - 117, 137, 138,
              149, 153, 169, 174, 190
    ch-tch, 156 - 157
    ff-ll-ss, 65, 74
    ge-dge, 142
    "i before e," 170, 172
    k, ck, 134 - 135
    suffixes, (VCV rule), 160 - 165, 203 - 206
    "twins," 125, 132
Suffixes, 133, 160 - 167, 191 - 193, 196 - 198
    ed, 166 - 167
    ky-key, 133
    spelling rules, 204 - 206
Syllable division, 109 - 110, 147
    long vowel in, 145 - 146
    compound words, 64
    consonant blends, 79

Syllables detached, consonant blends, 77 - 78
    consonant-vowel-consonant, 67 - 69
    "magic e", 91

t, 34
Tachistoscope, 62, 86
tch, as in catch, 156 - 157
th, hard, as in that, 53
   soft, as in thin, 60
tion, as in action, 173 - 174
Treasure chest, 12, 24
Trigraph, consonant, 156
Twins, rule of, 125, 132

u, as in up, 43
ue, as in rescue, 108, 175, 177
   as in true, 177, 184
ur, as in burn, 113, 117 - 118
us, 206

v, 57
Visual stimulus, 15

Vocabulary development, 191 - 202
Vowel digraphs
   See Digraphs
Vowels, 84
   before tion, 173
   long, in syllable division, 145 - 147
   y, as a vowel, 144

w, 54
wh, 55
Word cards, 14
Writing, 15
   lined paper, 11

x, 58

y, as in yes, 56
   as a vowel, 144
   plus affixes, 205

z, 59, 190